THE QUEEN'S FLIGHT

Vickers Vikings served The King's Flight and The Queen's Flight between 1946 and 1958.

THE QUEEN'S FLIGHT

FIFTY YEARS OF ROYAL FLYING

EDITED BY MICHAEL BURNS

FOREWORD BY HRH THE DUKE OF EDINBURGH

BLANDFORD PRESS
POOLE · NEW YORK · SYDNEY

First published in the UK 1986 by Blandford Press,
Link House, West Street, Poole, Dorset BH15 1LL

Distributed in Australia by
Capricorn Link (Australia) Pty Ltd,
PO Box 665, Lane Cove, NSW 2066

British Library Cataloguing in Publication Data

The Queen's flight : fifty years of royal flying
  1935-1985.
  1. Great Britain. *Royal Air Force. Queen's Flight*
  —History
  I. Burns, Michael
  358.4′4′0941   UG635.G7

ISBN 0 7137 1888 9

Typeset by Megaron Typesetting, Bournemouth, Dorset.

Printed in Great Britain by R. J. Acford Ltd., Chichester, Sussex.

CONTENTS

BUCKINGHAM PALACE.

Passenger flying was very much in its infancy when
the King's Flight was established in 1936. Those were
the days of Ford Trimotors, Handley-Page Hannibals,
Douglas DC3s and the Junkers 52. I flew in most of
those types and I well remember flying from Croydon to
Le Bourget in one of the Handley-Page 4-engined bi-planes.
It flew sedately at about 90 knots at 1,500ft and was very
comfortable indeed. However, for sheer luxury there was
nothing quite like the Empire Flying Boats. I flew back in
one from Athens to Poole in 1939, stopping the night in
Corfu and Marseilles. There was no question of jet-lag
in those spacious days.

My first experience of flying with the King's Flight
was in one of the Vikings. I made several flights to and
from Malta while I was stationed there with the Navy. I think
it was the possibility of getting my hands on one of these
aircraft that decided me to learn to fly myself.

I started in a Chipmunk at White Waltham but I also
used Smith's Lawn at Windsor which had originally been
cleared for the use of The Prince of Wales (later The Duke
of Windsor), and Bircham Newton near Sandringham.

From the Chipmunk I graduated to a Harvard and then
to an Oxford for twin-engine experience. Eventually 'Mouse'
Fielden succeeded in acquiring a de Havilland Dove for the
Flight which was put at my disposal. I thoroughly enjoyed
that aircraft and I was almost disappointed to have to transfer
to a Heron. However, the feeling soon passed as I found
the Heron just as pleasant to fly. I completed some quite
adventurous flights in the Heron. London to Accra in 1959 and
Bathurst (now Banjul) to Dar es Salaam in 1961, particularly
stick in my mind.

Meanwhile I had also learnt to fly a helicopter in 1955.
The first time I flew in one was in March 1953 during a visit to
the British Services in Germany. On that occasion it was
a Westland Dragonfly from Boscombe Down. In May of that year,
just before The Queen's Coronation, the Navy provided a
Sikorsky Whirlwind so that I could visit the Commonwealth and
Empire military contingents at Woolwich and Pirbright. This
was the first time that a helicopter had used the garden
at Buckingham Palace and it did not prove to be very popular
with 'the powers that be'.

The Flight had started to use helicopters in 1947.
I remember they flew the mail from Aberdeen to Balmoral,

but that did not last very long as any headwind made
them rather slower than a motor-car and bad weather
stopped them altogether.

By the time I had qualified the Flight had acquired
a piston-engined Westland Whirlwind. This was followed
by the turbine version and eventually by the current
Westland Wessex.

In my view flying a helicopter is the nearest thing to
true flying, since it is possible to take off and land
vertically and to move backwards and sideways as well as
forwards whenever you feel like it. With the limitations
imposed by present traffic problems, the helicopters have
given members of the Family the chance to accomplish a
great deal more in the course of a day.

It so happens that I enjoy flying and I have
frequently made use of the Andovers to undertake journeys
for which they were never intended. Flights across
the north Atlantic in winter via Iceland, Greenland and
Labrador can be spectacular under the Aurora Borealis.
It may take 9 days to get from London to Australia but it
is a marvellous experience. It must be about the only
time I ever arrived there as fresh as the proverbial daisy.

None of all this would have been possible without
the skill and proficiency of the Flight's engineers and
aircrews. The Flight's record of reliability cannot be
bettered by any commercial or military flying organisation
anywhere in the world. This is partly due to the fact
that it is organised in much the same way as the Royal
Yacht Service. Once posted to the Yacht or the Flight,
the majority can remain in their jobs until there is a
prior opportunity for promotion in the general service,
or until retirement. The experience built up under this
system is quite invaluable.

It is a happy coincidence that the introduction of
the BAe 146 into The Queen's Flight is due to take place
in its 50th anniversary year. I shall be sad to say
'good-bye' to the faithful Andovers, but I cannot wait
to get my hands on the new aircraft.

I am delighted that the story of this unique unit of
the RAF has been written. It has rendered quite exceptional
service to 3 Sovereigns and their families and I hope it
will continue to do so for many generations to come.

1986

The Duke of Edinburgh's personal de Havilland Heron C3, XH375, was on charge to The Queen's Flight from May 1955 to September 1964. He had become an enthusiast for the type after evaluating Heron G-AMTS on loan from de Havilland in January-April 1955.

EDITOR'S PREFACE

The de Havilland Heron C4 (farther) served The Queen's Flight from 1958 until replaced by the HSA Andover CC2 (nearer) from 1964. XS790 was the first Andover CC2 allocated to The Queen's Flight, on 10 July 1964.

This book has been written by members and ex-members of The Queen's Flight, to whom warmest thanks are due. In keeping with the *esprit de corps* of the Flight, it has been a team effort, but special mention should be made of Flight Sergeant Terry Harper RVM, who had the original idea for the book; of the Captain of The Queen's Flight, Air Vice-Marshal John Severne LVO, OBE, AFC, whose support and advice were freely given and greatly welcomed; of the Commanding Officer, Wing Commander Mike Schofield, in many ways the moving spirit behind the whole project; and of Squadron Leader Roger Bent, the Flight's Senior Engineering Officer, who co-ordinated the contributors with tireless efficiency and courtesy.

MICHAEL BURNS

1

A DAY IN THE LIFE
OF THE QUEEN'S FLIGHT

'Queen's Flight Operations, this is Kittyhawk One. How do you read me? Over.'

'Kittyhawk One, this is Queen's Flight Operations reading you loud and clear. Go ahead your message.'

'Operations, this is Kittyhawk One. We are unable to land at scheduled destination due to weather. Diverting instead to Edinburgh. Request you inform Royal Household, and arrange transport accordingly. ETA Edinburgh, fifteen minutes past the hour.'

Short, sharp, to the point; but where do you begin?

Seems like a normal bad-weather diversion until you look at the passenger list. Kittyhawk One is carrying four Royal and VIP passengers, including HRH Princess Anne, and the cars originally intended for their use are nearly sixty miles away; for the Operations (Ops) staff, it's another incident in an already full day.

Today, the day began for some of the staff at 3 am; there was a full programme of aircraft movements ahead and the first flight scheduled to depart at 7 am. At three o'clock in the morning there aren't too many people around to share your appreciation (or lack of it) of a new day – the only glimmer of life comes from the permanently manned security post where the RAF Police staff control entry to The Queen's Flight. In our Motor Transport Section the duty driver coughs and splutters almost as much as his vehicle as they launch into action; he is leaving to pick up the catering requirements and some other urgently needed items for today's Royal flights. He'll be back before 5 am, not quite full of the joys of spring, but at least more awake than the majority of the still-slumbering populace. In the Stewards' Bay, the stewards will cast expert eyes critically over the food before nodding their approval.

Shortly afterwards, several other sections will begin their day.

Next on the scene are 'the shift' (the first-line engineering personnel who are mainly concerned with handling aircraft movements and carrying out minor rectification work). The shift consists of about eight tradesmen, under the supervision of a Chief Technician, who report for duty this morning at 5 am to carry out 'Before-Flight' servicing on the Andover and Wessex aircraft which are assigned to Royal tasks today.

The Ops clerk checks in at 5.30 am and Ops will now be manned until the last aircraft is back, safely tucked-up, at 11.30 tonight. For Ops the work is not particularly physically hard, but like everyone else on The Queen's Flight, they are required to work carefully and diligently, but above all professionally and with a great degree of responsibility.

There are approximately 185 people on The Queen's Flight based at RAF Benson; every trade and profession from carpenter to fireman to the Duke of Edinburgh's personal pilot has a vital function to perform in the daily running of this unique unit. Even to mention briefly the role and tasks of each section would fill an encyclopaedia, so to illustrate the general link-up between various parts of the unit, let's concentrate on one aspect of today's busy programme – the flying task.

There are four Ops clerks, one of whom is the Corporal in charge, and they operate a shift system with two clerks always on duty during the hours from

Photographed in the quiet of dawn, the pristine hangar at Royal Air Force Benson, Oxfordshire, which is the home of The Queen's Flight. Three of the world's most immaculate aeroplanes and two of the world's most immaculate helicopters, the Royal Andovers and Wessex, await another day's arduous tasking.

One task under way. HM Queen Elizabeth The Queen Mother arriving for an engagement in Andover XS789. The other two Andovers may simultaneously be on tasks many miles away in the UK or thousands of miles away overseas.

8 am until 5 pm. Outside those times one man will usually cover all aircraft movements to and from The Queen's Flight. In a standard day, if such a thing exists, there will be up to fifty or sixty telephone calls to be made and probably twice as many received, all requiring action of some sort – even if it's only to say, 'Thank you for calling, I'll pass the message on.' On top of that, there will be several teleprinter messages to be sent out and again just as many, if not more, to action on receipt from literally anywhere in the world.

As well as 'flight following', that is the procedure of monitoring an aircraft's progress as it carries out a task hour by hour, there is also the flight-planning room to be run. Duties here include everything from collecting and displaying the local weather information for Benson and the surrounding area to the collation and recording of navigation warnings for the whole of the United Kingdom. These last duties are fairly standard throughout most flight-planning sections in the RAF, but it is the unique nature of the flying tasks (and the special passengers) and the consequent requirement for the unusual to become the norm that gives the job much of its interest.

The type of flight and area of operation will also affect greatly the amount of work to be done for each individual task. For example, a 'Royal flight' carrying a senior member of the Royal Family will require specific pre-flight handling, known as Purple Airspace notification. Flights for other members of the Royal

Family are known as 'Special flights' and these do not qualify for a Purple Airspace. A flight to, say, Africa, to check out or 'prove' airfields and facilities for a future Royal Tour, will require equally important but vastly different procedures and arrangements before the aircraft can leave the United Kingdom: such diverse items as diplomatic clearance – the permit to overfly or land in a foreign country – and airport handling requests, whereby an airline or aircraft handling agent is asked to arrange everything from the fuel for the aircraft to the overnight accommodation for the crew, will all be channelled through the Ops clerk.

But back to today, and of the five aircraft held on the Flight, four will be in use; one of the three Andovers is being serviced and will not be fit to fly for a few days yet. This aircraft has been on jacks since the servicing began three weeks ago; today the 'riggers' (airframe tradesmen) will be putting the final touches to the undercarriage system. At the same time, inside the aircraft, several other tradesmen will all be working towards the same goal – getting the aircraft back to its perfect flying condition by the target date, which seems to advance with ever-increasing haste. There will be interior furnishing workers replacing roofing panels, and radio technicians checking a particularly frustrating reception problem on one of the aircraft radios, whilst outside the aircraft, propulsion tradesmen will be methodically piecing together the port engine which has just been replaced. Near the nose of the aircraft one of the painters will be repairing a minor surface blemish on the paintwork. With all the modern technology available these days, it's heartening to see that all the traditional skills are not entirely dead – the painter uses a nail varnish brush (and a lot of expertise) to hide a small mark left by an unthinking hailstone. As the painter puts it, 'How dare they mark my beautiful skin' – it's almost as if it *were* his own skin involved. Of the other two Andovers, one is away with HRH The Duke of Edinburgh on an overseas tour and the other is scheduled to fly Princess Anne to Scotland. At the same time the two Wessex helicopters will be busy, one of them flying the Prince of Wales around the south-west of England on a two-day task, the other taking the Duke and Duchess of Kent to engagements in the Midlands and East Anglia.

Today is one of those typically British days with no two areas of the country sharing the same type of weather, so it's hardly surprising when the aircrews warn of 'possible changes to the programme'.

Just after 6 am, the first of the crews start to arrive; this is the crew of the first aircraft out, an Andover. There is an air of quiet efficiency surrounding the Ops room, probably more to do with the time of day than anything else, as crew and Ops clerk go about the business of preparing to commit aviation. The weather for departure, arrival and en route airfields is studied and commented upon. Grumbles of 'I suppose it'll be the co-pilot's landing, looking at this forecast' are met with 'If you're not careful, I'll make you do it asymmetric' (ie. landing with one engine throttled back simulating a power failure; practised, without passengers, on a regular basis).

Pride of purpose is reflected in the weekly washing and polishing given to each aircraft by all tradesmen of Sergeant and below in rank, sixty of whom take an hour of elbow-greasing to produce showroom finishes. An overall white polyurethane scheme replaced the earlier white upper and natural metal lower surfaces because the unpainted skin panels were wearing thin under the constant buffing.

The life-blood of aircrew and groundcrew alike, the first coffee, is quaffed in copious quantities, and slowly but very perceptibly the task comes ever-nearer to departure. By 6.30 am the aircraft will be towed out of the hangar to the accompaniment of much clanging of huge hangar doors and revving of the tractor engine, and cries of 'Brakes off!' 'Okay, brakes off!' in the ever-increasing brouhaha of the early day. Back in the Ops room the clerk is checking the airfield state with Air Traffic Control and confirming the departure details for the aircraft.

Out on the Andover's parking spot, 'the shift' have positioned the necessary ground support equipment such as fire extinguisher, aircraft steps and power-supply unit and have left the aircraft under the watchful eyes of our RAF Police staff. They will ensure that no unauthorised person attempts to approach the aircraft.

At seven o'clock on the dot, the whine of the starboard engine of XS793 heralds the start of Task 1246. The whine builds to an eardrum-piercing, high-pitched scream, then suddenly it fades, as the aircraft is taxied out to the runway for take-off. Its departure time is logged in the Ops room, and immediately it's time to start thinking about the next task; this one's the Prince of Wales' Wessex, due to depart at 8.30 am, and by 7.15 the crew are in Ops going through slightly different procedures for their departure. Early-morning fog could make things awkward at the pick-up point in London, so the Ops clerk is asked to check the latest actual weather at Heathrow and Northolt airports and also the serviceability state of all their approach and landing aids 'just in case we have to use them for a cloud-break of sorts'.

At 7.30 the pilot of the Wessex carries out a ground-run of the helicopter to check out the engines and systems (this is done one hour before departure time from Benson to allow time for any minor rectifications) while back in Ops the navigator is putting the finishing touches to his flight-planning for the task. By eight o'clock the majority of personnel from all the other trades have reported for work; there's no clocking in or out, but it soon becomes obvious if anyone is missing. The Corporal in charge of Ops has also come in and is quickly bringing himself up to date on the happenings of last night and this morning. The calm and peace of an hour ago is progressively eroded as phones start ringing, teleprinters begin their seemingly incessant chattering and the intercom box alternately bleeps then shouts as 'customers' check in.

Around mid-morning, all four aircraft are proceeding on task and messages, both verbal and printed, are flashing backwards and forwards through Ops. There are changes to the names of passengers expected to join the flight in Scotland. At the same time another crew, planning a future task, need to know if a particular route, over a foreign country distinctly 'cool' in its dealings with the UK, can be used or if the aircraft will need to be re-routed: a call from Ops to the Ministry of Defence does not produce the answer so a signal is hurriedly composed and sent off to the British Embassy in the capital, seeking their reassurance that the aircraft will be allowed to fly the requested route.

Along the corridor, the administrative staff in the General Office are quietly going about their business while next door to them, the Chief Clerk, an acknowledged mine of information on everything from AP 3392 (Manual of Personnel Administration – Pay and Personnel Documentation) to the Rules of Golf, is liaising by telephone with the RAF Personnel Management Centre at Innsworth, Gloucestershire, on behalf of a young airman who is shortly to be posted.

Just before lunch, an incoming signal to Ops informs us that the aircraft on the overseas tour has an engineering problem and some spares are urgently required at the next stop. First job is to tell the suppliers; they'll arrange the despatch of the spares once we've established the easiest and quickest means of getting them out there. A quick check on the airline computer terminal in Ops reveals that there's a civil flight leaving Heathrow tonight; however, the packaged spares must be at the airline's office within two hours. Tell the MT Section of the need for a vehicle to leave with the spares in half an hour. Next, signal back to the aircraft that spares are (hopefully) on their way and tell them not to panic – there's enough of that going on here!

Just when it all appears to have been sorted out, the phone rings. The brief respite over lunch has ended and the indigestion is about to start.

One of the helicopters is filing a Royal Low-Level Corridor violation. This means that an aircraft has strayed into the protected airspace surrounding the Royal helicopter and could have caused an incident. In this case there was no

Royal visits involve complex logistics and a contribution from many parties, all of whom are ultimately dependent upon The Queen's Flight. An example was this visit by HM The Queen to the Jaguar GR1 equipped squadrons (Nos. 41 and 54) at RAF Coltishall in 1983.

risk to Royal passenger or aircraft, but the matter has been taken up officially. What to do? Log the details and report the matter to several interested parties both inside and outside The Queen's Flight; the 'Adj' will take care of it from there, looking at aspects such as did/will the Press get hold of the correct story? Much to-ing and fro-ing over this one lasts well into the afternoon. We've changed shifts on the Ops clerk side at lunchtime so there's someone else to be briefed on the – as yet incomplete – day's events.

From here on, the rest of the day is plain sailing. Confirmation comes that the spares made it on time and are winging their way on board a southbound 747. Did we dare say plain sailing? Not quite. There's the little matter of a last-minute notice Royal task for a Wessex tomorrow. Most of the agencies concerned have closed for now, so we'll have to arrange as much of it as possible: everything from notifying the crew, who are still out in Norfolk with the Duke and Duchess of Kent to arranging to have the Royal route promulgated to all the many agencies involved, by signal and by telephone. Oh, and don't forget to tell the stewards and Security and so on and so on. . . .

Meanwhile, you're dying to know what happened to Kittyhawk One up at Edinburgh, aren't you? Well, as requested, the Royal Household was informed. There were no other cars anywhere near Edinburgh at that time, so could we help? Called the Station Commander at RAF Turnhouse, the military part of Edinburgh airport – could he possibly provide two staff cars and a baggage vehicle at short notice? Bit tricky, but yes, should be able to help with

HRH The Duke of Gloucester examining part of The Queen's Flight's comprehensive collection of national pennants, flown next to the standard of the Royal personage being carried when visiting a foreign country.

The rewards of service. A charming thank-you for the Commodore (in this case one of the Flight's Deputy Captains, Group Captain Jeremy Jones) from one of the youngest generation of Royal flyers, Prince William of Wales. Quite unprompted, Prince William toddled back to the steps and solemnly shook hands after the Andover had arrived at Aberdeen on 25 March 1985.

something. Any chance of a knighthood next time? No?, Oh well, we aim to please anyway. Aircraft landed safely, passengers driven off in a variety of charabancs, quick refuel, then aircraft lifts off into the murk and heads back to Benson.

Back at base, the engineers converge upon the Andover almost as soon as it stops, and the 'After-Flight' servicing and refuelling commences without delay. The aircraft has developed a slight autopilot malfunction, and a Corporal is despatched immediately to discuss the snag with the aircraft captain.

Having delivered the Duke and Duchess of Kent safely home, their Wessex flutters into view at Benson and shuts down near the hangar. It is due for a 'Primary' servicing (having completed 75 flying hours since the last one) this evening, so the engineers are delighted that the aircrew have no unserviceabilities to report which would add to their overnight workload. The helicopter cabin is unloaded by one of the General Duties tradesmen who will later clean the interior for tomorrow's flight, and then the refuelling tanker lumbers up, driven by the duty MT driver, and refuelling begins.

The Andover, meanwhile, has been brought into the hangar and cleaned. Its servicing is complete apart from the autopilot problem, which should be fixed within the hour. However, it also requires a 'role' change − a change of seat-fit for one of tomorrow's Royal flights − and once this has been completed, the aircraft will be inspected in microscopic detail both inside and out by one of the engineering management team to ensure that it is up to the immaculate standard required for tomorrow's flight.

After the refuel of the Wessex, various engineering checks are completed before the aircraft is towed into the hangar for the 75-hour servicing to begin. This will occupy the shift personnel until about 11 pm if no unexpected faults are discovered. Then, assuming the Andover has successfully passed its engineering inspection, the shift can knock off, leaving the hangar and aircraft secure in the care of the duty policemen.

Back in Ops, at around midnight, things are quietening down. Suddenly the teleprinter starts to chatter. Hope the duty driver's not sleeping *too* soundly − he'll love this one!

2

THE HISTORY OF
THE KING'S FLIGHT
AND THE QUEEN'S FLIGHT

THE BEGINNINGS

The Queen's Flight of today is descended from the personal flying unit established by the Prince of Wales at Northolt in 1929 which subsequently became The King's Flight in 1936. However, Royal flights and Royal aircraft go back much further than The King's Flight, for the history of Royal flying can be traced to 17 July 1917, when the Prince of Wales was taken up in France. He next flew on 16 September 1918 with Captain W.G. Barker in a Bristol Fighter of No. 139 Squadron when he visited the Italian front.

In March 1919 his brother, Prince Albert, took a flying course at Waddon Lane, Croydon. Two Avro 504s from the Air Council Communication Squadron were allocated for the course. He received his wings as a certified pilot on 31 July 1919 and his permanent commission as a Squadron Leader was gazetted the following day. He was thus the first member of the Royal Family to become a fully qualified pilot and is the only British Sovereign to have achieved this distinction. These activities were short-lived, however, for after the war the Prince of Wales again met Barker, now a Major with the VC, and flew with him in a Sopwith Dove. Barker, still recovering from wounds received on the Western Front, piloted with one arm in a sling, and when The King heard of the risks involved, he advised his sons not to fly again.

It took some years for King George V's attitude to change, and it was not until 1928 that the Prince of Wales again took up flying seriously, although in the meantime he had patronised some of the early airline services to the Continent. On 27 April 1928, the Prince flew for thirty minutes at Northolt in a Bristol Fighter of No. 24 Squadron, piloted by Flying Officer G.C. Stemp, and two weeks later that unit's establishment was increased by the addition of a Bristol Fighter annotated 'for Special Service', a temporary allocation pending delivery of two specially-equipped Westland Wapiti 1As. The first official conveyance of a member of the Royal Family by air came on 27 May 1928, when Flight Lieutenant J.S. Don flew the Prince of Wales from Scarborough to Bircham Newton in one of the Bristol Fighters.

Two Wapitis, J9095 and J9096, arrived at Northolt in June 1928 and were soon in demand for a variety of VIPs, even though their 'VIP' fit still included an open cockpit rather than an enclosed cabin. The Prince made a number of journeys in J9095, flown by Don. However, his interest in flying was soon such that in September 1929 he forsook the Wapitis and bought an aeroplane of his own, a de Havilland Gipsy Moth, G-AALG, which was finished in the red and blue colours of the Brigade of Guards, colours which have now become traditional in one form or another for Royal aircraft. He arranged for Don to teach him to fly and on 17 November 1929, after some thirty hours dual, most of it cross-country, the Prince flew a short solo sortie at Northolt in Gipsy Moth G-AAKV. However, by this time it was becoming increasingly difficult for Don to carry out his Squadron duties as well as overseeing the operation of the Prince's private aeroplane, so it was suggested that the Prince should appoint his own personal pilot. He chose for the task Flight Lieutenant E.H. Fielden (the late Air Vice-Marshal Sir Edward Fielden GCVO, CB, DFC, AFC), who had recently been transferred to the Reserve of Royal Air Force Officers. Fielden took full charge of the Prince's private aeroplane, which was kept at Northolt. He flew it at all times and was responsible for its maintenance. The Wapiti J9095 continued to be used occasionally and three RAF pilots, headed by

HRH The Prince of Wales (later King Edward VIII) in the cockpit of a Bristol F2B Fighter of No. 139 Squadron at Villaverla, Italy, on 27 September 1918. The pilot was Captain S. Dalrymple RAF, who took the Prince on a fifteen-minute flight. The Prince was a Major in the Grenadier Guards, serving in Italy on the Staff of XIV Army Corps. No. 139 Squadron was part of the Corps' air component.

HRH Captain Prince Albert
(second from left), who later
became King George VI, was
flown from England to France
in a Handley Page 0/400
bomber by Major Greig RAF
(third from left) on 31 October
1918. They are seen in flying
kit before take-off.

The Prince of Wales took a
keen interest in aviation and is
seen boarding the prototype
Sopwith Dove, a two-seater
conversion of the Pup fighting
scout, at Hounslow on 10 May
1919. The first post-war
sporting aeroplane, it had been
given its maiden flight that
morning by Major Barker VC,
DSO, MC. He then took up the
Prince and performed several
stunts much to the young
Prince's liking, but not to the
King's, who curtailed his heir's
flying activities for several
years. Barker was still
recovering from severe wounds
received in a VC-winning
single-handed combat against
impossible odds over France,
and was still in plaster! The
King was naturally concerned
that his heir was being flown by
a less than 100 per cent able-
bodied pilot, in stunts, in a
prototype.

Squadron Leader Don, were authorised to fly it carrying the Prince of Wales and other members of the Royal Family.

In 1930, the Prince of Wales bought another DH60 Gipsy Moth, G-ABCW, to supplement G-AALG, and when this new addition suffered an unspecified mishap on 18 July 1930, it was quickly replaced by a third Gipsy Moth, G-ABDB. A further purchase was a cabin monoplane, DH80A Puss Moth G-ABBS. The Prince continued to call on No. 24 Squadron to fly him on some official visits, and for this the Wapitis were replaced in 1930 by Fairey 111Fs: K1115 (the Royal aircraft) and J9061. The Prince sought every opportunity to indulge his love of flying, using a great variety of aircraft and flying-boats. In 1931, he hired a Westland Wessex for his holiday in France, gaining first-hand experience of operating a large, multi-engined aeroplane.

(Text continues on page 28)

Prince Albert gained his wings as a serving officer in the RAF in 1919, flying an Avro 504J, C4451, the first aircraft allocated specifically for a Royal task. The 504J was developed as a trainer from the 504A fighting machine and was used at the RFC and RAF training schools, where it was enormously popular.

Bristol F2B Fighter J8430 was the first aircraft officially allotted for Royal engagements. It had a modified rear cockpit with a windscreen and was fitted with Handley Page slats in the upper wing leading edge. Held by No. 24 (Communications) Squadron, it was finished in standard RAF aluminium dope with the Squadron's red chevron emblem on the fin. The Prince of Wales is seen departing for Northolt from Mousehold aerodrome, Norwich, after inspecting the Norfolk and Norwich Aero Club, on 30 May 1928.

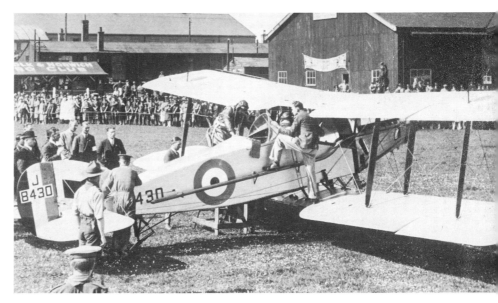

In June 1928, two Wapiti IAs, J9095 and J9096, replaced F2B J8439 as the aircraft held by No. 24 Squadron for Royal flights. Like the F2B, the Wapitis were in standard service finish — overall aluminium dope with dark green upper decking — and carried No. 24 Squadron's red chevron, with the addition of the Prince's Group Captain's rank pennant painted on the outboard wing struts.

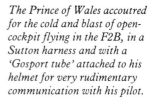

The Prince of Wales accoutred for the cold and blast of open-cockpit flying in the F2B, in a Sutton harness and with a 'Gosport tube' attached to his helmet for very rudimentary communication with his pilot.

The Prince usually flew in Wapiti IA J9095, piloted by Squadron Leader Don, with Flight Lieutenant Stemp flying J9096, carrying whomever accompanied the Prince or as escort if the Prince was alone. J9095 and J9096 were specially built for the Prince with Jupiter VI engines, Fairey-Reed metal propellers, a VIP rear cockpit and metal rear fuselage panels.

DH60M Gipsy Moth G-AALG, with the latest in cockpit luxury, pneumatic upholstery, was the first aircraft personally owned by the Prince of Wales (seen left). It was fully dual-control equipped and the Prince learnt to fly in this aircraft, tutored by Squadron Leader Don, with the permission of the King. For Royal flying, however, Don flew the aircraft. On 16 November 1929, Don made a forced landing in G-AALG; the axle was broken in this, the first Royal flying accident, but neither Don nor the Prince was hurt. G-AALG was finished, as were all the Prince's privately owned aircraft, in the red and blue colours of the Brigade of Guards, with whom the Prince had served during the Great War.

Upon arrival at Andover in Fairey IIIF K1115 on 13 August 1930 while visiting various RAF bases during the 1930 Air Exercises, the Prince of Wales was greeted by Air Vice-Marshal Sir John Steele, KBE, CB, CMB, the AOC Wessex Area, who was commanding the 'Blueland' forces during the Exercises. The first buzzing of a Royal aircraft took place during that day when a squadron of 'Redland' Siskin fighters intercepted the IIIF over their sector while it was making for 'Blueland'. The IIIF's pilot, Don, unobligingly kept flying straight and level, adhering to the strict orders laid down by C-in-C Inland Area for Royal flights.

K1115 and J9061 were the initial two specially-fitted Fairey IIIF's operated by No. 24 Squadron.

DH80A Puss Moth G-ABBS was the Prince of Wales' first cabin monoplane. His other DH80A, G-ABFV, was sent, crated aboard HMS Eagle, to South America for his 1931 Royal tour.

The Prince of Wales leaves Westland Wessex G-ABVB. When the need for a larger, longer-range aircraft than the Puss Moth became apparent, the Wessex was seen as ideal and the Prince viewed the prototype at Westland's Yeovil works in 1930.

Tomtit G-AALL, loaned to the Prince of Wales for the 1930 King's Cup Air Race.

The Prince of Wales used Wessex G-ABEG on loan from Westlands on several occasions during the early 1930s, notably for his tour of France and holiday in Cannes from 18 August to 19 September 1931. It was flown by Flight Lieutenant E.H. Fielden with Mr T. Jenkins as ground engineer.

'THE ROYAL FLIGHT' AT HENDON

In 1931, the Prince of Wales' private aircraft had moved from Northolt to Hendon. Since the Prince held the RAF rank of Air Chief Marshal, the aircraft were housed in the Display hangar 'under the same conditions which permitted serving officers to maintain private aeroplanes'. Servicing, inspection and maintenance remained the responsibility of Flight Lieutenant Fielden and the aircraft were registered in his name, although they were in every way the property of the Prince of Wales. Since they had the numerical strength of a Royal Air Force flight, they soon became known collectively as 'The Royal Flight'. This title was quite unofficial, for such a unit was not established for a further six years, but the style 'The Prince of Wales' Hangar' was in semi-official use by 1932.

The original Puss Moth, G-ABBS, was replaced during 1931 by a third Puss Moth, G-ABNN, which set the style followed on all but one of the Prince's subsequent aircraft, that of having the last two registration letters the same. The fourth and final Puss Moth, G-ABRR, was obtained in September 1931.

In 1931, the Prince of Wales carried out a tour of South America using Puss

Flight Lieutenant E.H. Fielden in the casual flying clothing of the day, a Norfolk jacket, steps into the Comper Swift, G-ABWW, which was entered by the Prince of Wales in the 1932 King's Cup race. Fielden came second at a speed of 155.75 mph.

David   G.R.I.   Bertie

July 6ᵗʰ 1935.

A unique signed portrait of three British Kings in Royal Air Force uniform.

Moth G-ABFV, which had been shipped out in HMS *Eagle*. During this tour, on 9 April, HRH carried out the first Royal deck landing when he flew on to the deck of HMS *Eagle* in a Fairey 111F off the coast of Rio de Janeiro.

By December 1932, the fleet comprised three generations of the de Havilland Moth family – two DH60 Gipsy Moths, one DH80 Puss Moth and a DH83 Fox Moth. The Prince, in consultation with Fielden, reviewed his aircraft requirements as the existing machines were too small to carry more than an ADC and valet. On 15 May 1933, Fielden took delivery of a twin-engined Vickers Viastra X, G-ACCC, which was the first aircraft specifically ordered and built for a member of the Royal Family. A new DH84 Dragon, G-ACGG, which was delivered on 12 June 1933, proved popular and successful and remained with the fleet until February 1935, when it was sold to Mr R. Shuttleworth, the founder of the Shuttleworth Collection of historic aeroplanes and motor cars. The Viastra, too, was sold in March 1935, having flown less

DH83 Fox Moth G-ACDD, procured in exchange for the smaller Puss Moth G-ABNN in December 1932. It also was finished in the Brigade of Guards' colours – red and blue, with a silver cheat line – and followed the practice on Royal aircraft of having the last two letters of the registration the same.

Fielden lands the Gipsy Swift in a perfect three-point landing. G-ABWW had a de Havilland Gipsy III engine in place of the standard Pobjoy but, apart from power-plant and fuselage nose, was generally identical to the Pobjoy-engined CLA-7 Swift.

than 10 hours in the previous year, and for a short time the Prince was then without an aircraft of his own. However, orders had been placed with de Havilland, and a pair of DH89 Dragon Rapides were soon delivered, G-ACTT on 27 April 1935 and G-ADDD on 8 June. An extensive flying programme had been envisaged for the summer of 1935 in connection with King George V's Jubilee celebrations, but once again there was found to be insufficient work for two aeroplanes, and by October 1935 G-ACTT was being offered for sale, having flown only fifty-one hours.

The Prince of Wales' twin-engined Vickers Type 259 Viastra MkX, G-ACCC, arriving at Brooklands. Brooklands was famous for its racing track, whose banking can be seen in the background, and as an aviation centre. The Viastra's design was unusual in that the airframe was stressed to allow any of single, twin or tri-engined versions. It was built at the Woolston, Southampton, works of Vickers-Supermarine. It spanned 70 feet and cruised at 130 mph. Its normal range of 700 miles could be increased to 1,050 miles with overload tanks.

The Prince of Wales is greeted upon arrival at Brooklands while Fielden steps from the Viastra, with Vickers' hangar in the background. The Viastra was the first special version of an aeroplane ordered for a member of the Royal Family. It met the requirement for an aircraft capable of carrying a Royal entourage in safety and comfort at fair speed over long ranges, and of acting as a flagship. The Wessex had been a useful study. Fielden assessed the types available and recommended the Viastra, which had been proven by Australian Airways. The Prince's aircraft was ordered on 3 November 1932 at a cost of £4,250. It was given its Certificate of Airworthiness on 16 May 1933.

DH84 Dragon G-ACGG photographed in flight over the south coast near Hastings. The aircraft was owned by the Prince of Wales from 12 June 1933 until it was sold on 5 February 1935 to Richard O. Shuttleworth, who later founded the famous vintage aircraft collection at Old Warden, Bedfordshire. The sale of G-ACGG partly financed the purchase of two DH89s, the DH89 being an improved DH84.

'Mouse' Fielden photographed in typical pose during the 1930s.

The Prince of Wales bought two DH89 Dragon Rapides as a replacement for the Viastra. G-ACTT (DH No. 6257) was delivered on 27 April 1935 but, after flying only fifty-one hours on Royal business, it was sold to Olley Air Services on 24 February 1936 as there was little call for two DH89s.

The Prince of Wales conversing with 'Mouse' Fielden – about flying, judging by the hand gestures – with G-ACGG behind them.

DH89 Dragon Rapide G-ADDD (DH No. 6283) was delivered on 8 June 1935, and was sold by Fielden after a total of 194 hours in Royal service to Western Airways Ltd for £3,345 on its owner's behalf.

In January 1936, the Prince of Wales became King Edward VIII. He is seen after arriving in Rapide G-ADDD at RAF Mildenhall on 8 July 1936 to review the Handley Page Heyfords of Nos 38 and 99 Squadrons and the Hawker Hinds of No. 40 Squadron. This was G-ADDD's most onerous day, for the King, accompanied by his brother, the Duke of York, visited several RAF stations by air: Northolt, Duxford, Wittering and Mildenhall, finishing off with a visit to A & AEE Martlesham Heath to see the Spitfire and Hurricane prototypes.

THE FIRST BRITISH MONARCH TO FLY

When George V died on 20 January 1936, the Prince of Wales became King Edward VIII. He had to attend the Accession Council in London the following day and Fielden flew The King and the Duke of York from Bircham Newton to Hendon in the Rapide, G-ADDD, which was the only aircraft now operated by The King. Since neither George V nor Queen Mary ever flew, this was the first occasion that a British monarch had taken to the air.

The King and the Duke of York inspect the men and Heyfords (looking 'like the Forth Bridge') of No. 38 Squadron at RAF Mildenhall on 8 July 1936.

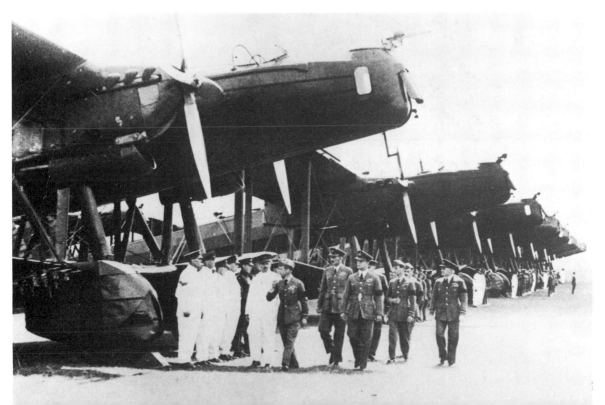

THE KING'S FLIGHT IS FORMED

As a Marshal of the Royal Air Force, The King was entitled to a communications-type aircraft for use on offical occasions, so the Air Ministry agreed to meet the cost of any replacement for his Dragon Rapide and, as from 1 April 1936, to finance the support of the Royal aircraft. This led in June to the institution of The King's Flight and on 21 July it formed officially; on the same day, Flight Lieutenant Fielden was nominated as an Equerry in Waiting with the appointment of Captain of The King's Flight. Fielden was promoted to Wing Commander and the two civilian ground engineers, T. Jenkins and R.T. Hussey, were given appropriate RAF NCO status; the fourth member of the Flight was Mr Peskett, the Captain's secretary.

King Edward abdicated in favour of the Duke of York on 11 December 1936. The new King retained Fielden's services as Captain of The King's Flight, but for the moment the Flight was without aircraft since the Dragon Rapide, G-ADDD, was the personal property of the former King and as such, it was sold in May 1937. The search for a new aircraft was now urgent.

Early in 1937, interest centred on the Airspeed Envoy, and although Fielden considered it too small for the requirements of The King's Flight, it was the most suitable replacement available; it had the additional advantage that a military version was to enter RAF service as the Oxford. Accordingly, in March 1937, Air Ministry Specification No. 6/37 was drawn up to cover 'the Airspeed Envoy III aircraft for The King's Flight, and to define certain special requirements which are necessary'. This was the first official specification to be made for a Royal aircraft and the aeroplane which emerged, G-AEXX, was the first Royal aircraft to be financed from public funds.

The elegant Airspeed Envoy III G-AEXX was the first publicly-funded Royal aircraft and the first covered by an official Air Ministry Specification, 6/37, which called for a radio and operator to be carried, additional fuel-tanks to be installed in the wings and Fairey-Reed metal propellers to be fitted. The Envoy was also procured by the RAF as the military Oxford.

The pilot's compartment of G-AEXX. In order to accommodate a radio and its operator, the compartment's rear bulkhead was moved back nine inches. Nevil Shute, founder and joint managing director of Airspeed Ltd, wrote in his autobiography, Slide Rule, about the purchase of the Envoy by the Flight: 'With this order, I think Airspeed reached the peak of its career. Whatever the profit and loss account might show, no company could receive a higher endorsement of the quality of its products than we had received. We might continue to do as well technically; we could hardly do better.'

G-AEXX was finished in blue and red with silver wings. The Captain, Fielden, in conjunction with Air Ministry officials, was responsible for the cabin furnishing and colour scheme. The Envoy underwent flight testing against its specification at A & AEE Martlesham Heath between 21 April and 3 May 1937.

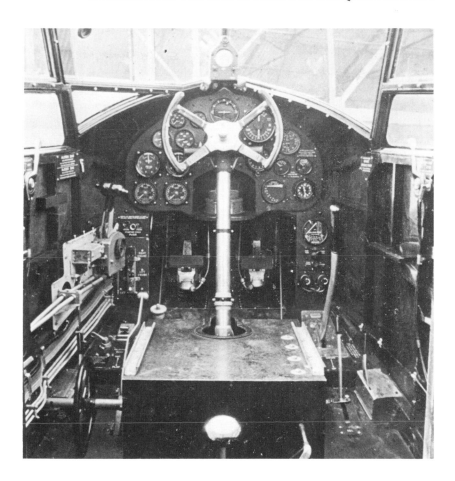

It is noteworthy that the Envoy had to meet the military requirements of the Air Ministry Directorates of Technical Development and Aeronautical Inspection, as well as satisfying the British Civil Airworthiness Requirements – and, in addition, being fully satisfactory to the Captain of The King's Flight. These multiple standards have been applied to all subsequent peacetime aircraft of The King's Flight and The Queen's Flight.

After the Envoy had passed its service acceptance trials at Martlesham Heath, Wing Commander Fielden collected it from the Airspeed works at Portsmouth on 7 May 1937 and flew it to Hendon, where it was officially allotted to No. 24 (Communications) Squadron, for use by The King's Flight. The Air Ministry had suggested that, since the Envoy was to be maintained from Service sources,

King George VI leaving the cabin of the Envoy, whose door was positioned conveniently over the wing.

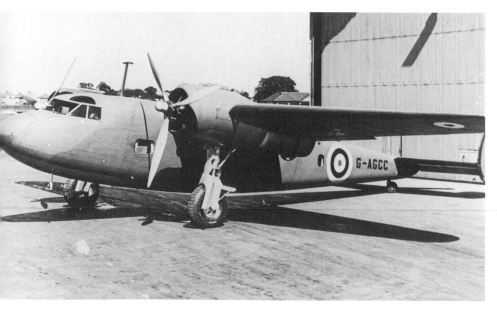

The King's Flight was allocated one of the three VIP DH95 Flamingoes procured by the Air Ministry, G-AGCC. The Flamingo was designed as a medium-range civil airliner and had been suggested as a suitable transport for the King in early 1939. The Air Ministry had ordered a troop transport version, the Hertfordshire, but abandoned it after initial evaluation. G-AGCC was camouflaged in the standard early-war Dark Earth/Dark Green/Sky Type S pattern, initially with roundels in six positions. It seems likely that subsequently, the roundels were removed and the wartime civil tricolour bars were painted on the fuselage.

the servicing crew should be put into uniform and the aircraft should become a military one, bearing the serial number L7270. These measures Fielden forestalled for as long as possible, and the aircraft retained its civil registration, G-AEXX, throughout its service on the Flight. Meanwhile, as ever, Fielden was on the lookout for a larger and potentially safer aeroplane for The King, and in 1938 he suggested the de Havilland Flamingo, a medium-range civil airliner which, as the Hertfordshire, was to be ordered for the RAF. As war became imminent, however, it was decided that the King should have an aircraft with defensive armament, and the choice fell on the Lockheed Hudson, descendant of the Super Electra airliner.

On 4 August 1939, therefore, Hudson N7263 arrived at Hendon to replace

King George VI leaving Flamingo G-AGCC after having been shown over it by Geoffrey de Havilland at the manufacturers' works at Hatfield on 15 August 1940. G-AGCC was fitted out to de luxe standards, with two cabins and re-positioned windows. There were so few in service, however, that the King became concerned that its operations might be placing a strain upon support resources and it was passed to No. 24 Squadron on 14 February 1942.

The Duke of Kent leaving Lockheed Hudson N7263 of The King's Flight. The Hudson met the need for a larger aircraft, with armament – the Boulton Paul turret equipped with twin .303-in Brownings is seen here. Fielden had earlier investigated procuring a Lockheed Electra airliner and thus, as a military development of the Super Electra airliner, the Hudson was a logical choice; no British aircraft adequately met the demands. A British Purchasing Commission (Air) in the USA had ordered 200 Hudsons in 1938, and N7263 was allocated to The King's Flight for modification directly upon arrival at Lockheed's UK depot at Speke airfield.

the Envoy, which in any case had become too small to accommodate comfortably the number of passengers and the amount of luggage now required. The Envoy had operated satisfactorily for more than two years, the only incident being late in its King's Flight career when, in July 1939, a wheel bogged down on take-off from Aberdeen with the Duke of Kent on board and considerable damage was done. The Envoy was then returned to its ostensible owners, No. 24 Squadron, now at Northolt, at last bearing its military serial number, L7270.

The Hudson, officially known as the Hudson (Long Range), had been extensively modified internally, both to improve passenger comfort and to provide fuel tankage for a range of 3,000 miles, which was now an official requirement. The aircraft retained its Boulton Paul upper turret with twin .303 Browning machine-guns, and relinquished the now traditional red, blue and silver paint scheme in favour of standard RAF camouflage with no distinctive marking other than its serial number. Fielden did not particularly like the Hudson, pointing out that it could carry but one passenger over the target range, and proposed that the Flight should acquire the two de Havilland Albatross prototypes, G-AEVV and G-AEVW. This proposal was not taken up.

BENSON

On the outbreak of war, it was suggested that The King's Flight should be transferred from Hendon, which was both busy and vulnerable, and be re-housed outside the London area. Fielden proposed a move to Smith's Lawn, in

Avro Tutor K6120 was on the strength of The King's Flight from 1 January 1940 until the Flight disbanded. It is the only King's or Queen's Flight aircraft of which no photograph is known to exist.

Windsor Great Park, from where he had flown many times in the early days with the Prince of Wales, but this move was not approved by the Air Ministry and in September 1939, the Flight made its new home at Benson, Oxfordshire, as a lodger unit of No. 12 OTU. In March 1940, the strength of the Flight was increased by the attachment of a Percival Q6, P5634, from Northolt for the use of AOC-in-C Bomber Command. In September of that year came the delivery of the latest Royal aircraft, a de luxe version of the de Havilland DH95 Flamingo. This aircraft was initially given the serial number R2766 but, as it was considered that a civil registration might facilitate the aeroplane's passage through neutral countries in the event of an emergency, it was registered as G-AGCC, although retaining its RAF roundels and camouflage.

THE KING'S FLIGHT DISBANDS

The aircraft of The King's Flight saw little use in 1941, particularly as the unarmed Flamingo would have required a fighter escort and, being an unfamiliar aircraft, could have been in some danger from the home defences. The King was concerned at the difficulties of operating the Flamingo and felt that his aircraft could be put to better use in normal service, so The King's Flight was disbanded as a separate unit. The Flight was officially absorbed by No. 161 Squadron at Newmarket on 14 February 1942, with Wing Commander Fielden commanding the new squadron but retaining his appointment as Captain of The King's Flight. The Flight personnel and aircraft were gradually dispersed and finally, in June, the Royal Hudson N7263 joined Fielden on No.

The immaculate, natural metal Royal Douglas Dakota Mk IV, KN386, at Prague in 1945 contrasting with the weathered RAF Dakotas and Short Stirlings on the pan. KN386 bore the Transport Command badge on the nose.

161 Squadron at Tempsford; this aircraft continued to be flown on Special Duties Operations throughout the war. As a Group Captain, Fielden became Tempsford's Station Commander.

With the disbandment of The King's Flight, arrangements for Royal flying reverted to No. 24 Squadron, still operating as a VIP transport unit from Northolt. The King was impressed by a flight in a Dakota during his visit to Italy, and it was decided to allot one for future Royal flights. Dakota Mk IV KN386 was selected for The King and it joined No. 24 Squadron at Hendon in June 1945.

Late in 1945, it was represented to The King that in coming years, Royal travel by air over long distances would become as natural as travel by car over short distances so, in early 1946, The King formally approved the reconstruction of The King's Flight, confirming Fielden, now an Air Commodore, in the appointment of Captain of The King's Flight. As his deputy and RAF Commanding Officer of the Flight, Fielden selected a New Zealander, Wing Commander E.W. Tacon DSO, DFC, AFC.

THE SOUTH AFRICAN TOUR

The King's Flight officially re-formed at Benson on 1 May 1946, and it was hoped that it would be manned and equipped to establishment by 1 August in preparation for the forthcoming Royal Visit to the Union of South Africa. The intended aircraft establishment was one Avro York to VVIP specification and three Vickers Vikings (one for The King, one for The Queen and and one for the groundcrew) but by mid-May, the York proposal had been dropped in favour of a fourth Viking in freighter/workshop fit. It was hoped that the normal

The Queen's Vickers Viking C2, VL247, was identical to the King's and was crewed in 1946 by: Squadron Leader H.F. Payne AFC, pilot; Flight Lieutenant P.G. Tilbrook, co-pilot; Flight Lieutenant A. Knapper AFC, navigator; and Flight Lieutenant D.J. Dartmouth, signals.

*Avro York MW140
Endeavour was lent to The
King's Flight in January-
February 1948 for the proving
flight to Ceylon (Sri Lanka)
for the King's Far East tour,
which was subsequently
cancelled.*

passenger aircraft would be available by July for crew training and route proving, and the other three special aircraft by November; to this end, BEA were persuaded to give up two of their early places on the production line, being recompensed by aircraft of the standard RAF order. In the event, the first of the special order, the normal passenger aircraft VL245, was collected from Wisley on 11 August 1946.

Another early addition to the establishment was a de Havilland Dominie, RL951, which was collected from Dumfries on 15 July 1946. It was used for communications purposes until it was written off in an accident at Mount Farm, just north of Benson, on 11 November 1946, fortunately with no injury to the crew.

Two standard Vikings were delivered to Benson to help in working up the Flight. The remainder of the special Vikings soon followed, all arriving by January 1947. By February, the fleet of four special aircraft had established their base for the Royal Tour at Brooklyn Air Base, near Cape Town. The Vikings performed faultlessly during the long tour, taking The King and Queen, together with the two Princesses, to various parts of the Union and the Rhodesias, flying a total of 160,000 miles without incident, more about this tour will be found in Chapter 10.

After their return to Benson, the Vikings were regularly used for a number of years on Royal visits, giving largely trouble-free service except for one mishap. On 12 September 1947, whilst the Royal Family were in residence at Balmoral, VL245 took off from Aberdeen for Benson after the daily official mail delivery, developed engine trouble (a runaway propeller) and force-landed in a field, demolishing a stone wall in the process. Considerable repairs were required and the aircraft never returned to King's Flight service, being replaced in July 1948 by two standard RAF Vikings, experience having shown that ideally five Vikings were required for long tours such as the previous visit to South Africa and the projected trip to Australia and New Zealand.

THE FIRST HELICOPTERS

Although they proved unfortunate for the Vikings, the summer 1947 mail deliveries had been helpful in giving The King's Flight its first experience of helicopter operations. Two Hoverfly Mk 1s were borrowed from the Royal Navy in August and flown to Dyce, whence they were used to shuttle the mail to Balmoral and back.

Meanwhile, the Vikings had been used extensively in November 1947 for flights in connection with the wedding of Princess Elizabeth and Prince Philip. The Avro York proposal re-appeared briefly in 1948 and in fact, The King's Flight borrowed one example, MW140, from Bassingbourn in January 1948 for two proving flights to Ceylon. The exercise was not repeated, however, and the Flight continued to use the shorter-range Viking.

Lent to The King's Flight by the Royal Navy in August 1947, two Sikorsky Hoverfly Mk 1 helicopters, KL106 and KK973, were used for shuttle-service mail deliveries from the nearest practical airfield, Dyce, to Balmoral, where they used a cricket pitch in the castle's grounds as a landing field.

On 31 January 1952, Princess Elizabeth and the Duke of Edinburgh flew out of London airport in BOAC Argonaut Atlanta *— a Canadair C-4 — to begin a tour of East Africa. While the Royal couple were in East Africa, the King died. The Argonaut conveyed Queen Elizabeth II and the Duke of Edinburgh from Entebbe to England on 7 February 1952, where she was met by bare-headed Winston Churchill and Clement Attlee.*

HRH Prince Charles and HRH Princess Anne arriving at London airport on 9 June 1955 after their first flight. The details of this conversation were not recorded . . .

THE FIRST CIVIL CHARTERS

When Princess Elizabeth and Prince Philip flew to Montreal on 8 October 1951, it was the first-ever crossing of the Atlantic by air by a member of the Royal Family. The aircraft was the BOAC Stratocruiser *Canopus*, captained by O.P. Jones, the famous Imperial Airways pioneer. A civil aircraft was again used for the East Africa tour of 1952; it was during this tour that Princess Elizabeth heard of the death of her father. These flights marked a turning point for The King's Flight, for in the future, long-range Royal flights would largely be carried out by civil operators, leaving the Flight to concentrate on short and medium-range journeys — although this arrangement was not to be reached without much discussion.

THE QUEEN'S FLIGHT

When The Queen acceded to the throne on 6 February 1952, The King's Flight was still operating the Vikings, although the pressure of work was by now much less than in previous years. This led to the suggestion that, on the grounds of efficiency and economy, The King's Flight should cease to exist and that the task of Royal flying should be carried out by BEA, BOAC and the RAF, as appropriate, co-ordinated by the Air Equerry with a small staff. A committee, comprising senior officials of the Royal Household, the Treasury, the Air Ministry and the Ministry of Civil Aviation, was formed to discuss the suggestion, and the outcome was a system which, with some amendments, has operated ever since: The King's Flight, re-named The Queen's Flight on 1

August 1952, would continue as before, and the Ministry of Civil Aviation would arrange the provision of civil aircraft when those of The Queen's Flight were unsuitable for a particular task.

THE DUKE OF EDINBURGH LEARNS TO FLY

In May 1952, whilst these discussions were in progress, Prince Philip decided to take a course of flying instruction. He felt strongly that he should be taught to fly by the RAF, so a small flying unit with one Chipmunk was set up at White Waltham under the aegis of Home Command. His Royal Highness's instructor was Flight Lieutenant Caryl Gordon. In June 1953, de Havilland Devon VP961 arrived at White Waltham, where for several years it saw regular use for training and communications flights. However, it was soon found that the Devon was not big enough to carry more than a few staff and their baggage, so an order was placed for the larger, four-engined de Havilland Heron, to be designated Prince Philip's personal aircraft.

By December 1953, the Queen had agreed to the carriage in The Queen's Flight's aircraft of certain Government Ministers and Service Chiefs of Staff. Fielden was now putting forward, to replace the obsolescent Vikings, a firm requirement for one de Havilland Heron series II, as Prince Philip's personal aircraft, to be introduced in March 1954; one Vickers Viscount in VIP fit, to be delivered in June 1954; and two Vickers Viscounts to VVIP specification, to be ready by August 1954 and March 1955. In due course, Fielden altered his

Two DH Chipmunk T10s were allocated to The Queen's Flight, WP912 and WP861, for Prince Philip's primary flying training. They were based at White Waltham.

North American Harvards FX459 and KF729 were allocated for the Duke of Edinburgh's flying tuition at White Waltham. It is the only Harvard to have borne five-star insignia, denoting a Marshal of the Royal Air Force. The Duke is seen talking with his instructor, Flight Lieutenant Caryl R. Gordon.

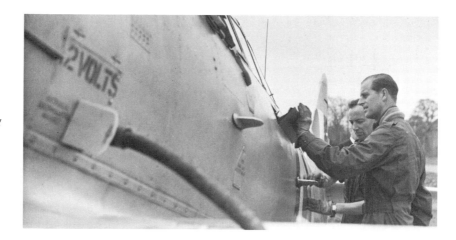

The Duke of Edinburgh flying Harvard XF729 over Windsor Castle. He first flew solo, in a Chipmunk at White Waltham, on 20 December 1952. The Duke won his wings in exactly the same manner as any other ab initio *student pilot. The Chief of Air Staff, Air Chief Marshal Sir William Dickson, presented him with his wings at Buckingham Palace on 8 May 1953.*

Overleaf: Four of the aircraft used by Prince Philip during his flying training formate over Windsor Castle: DH Chipmunk T10 ab initio trainer (WP912 and WP861 were used); NA Harvard advanced trainer (FX459 and XF729 were used); Airspeed Oxford V4204, primary twin-engined trainer; and DH Devon VP961, used for advanced twin-engined training.

requirements to suit the ever-changing work-load and climate of Air Ministry opinion, and in December 1954, having secured Prince Philip's agreement to his Heron being used by other members of the Royal Family (subject to his own overriding requirement), he suggested that one Viscount could possibly do the work of all the Vikings. The eventual establishment of The Queen's Flight would then have been one Viscount 700D, one Viking VVIP, one Heron and two Westland Whirlwind Mk 2 helicopters. However, even this much pruned request was turned down by the Treasury and eventually the whole Viscount project fell through. One of the officers on the Flight at that time vividly recalls the decision and its consequences.

In 1953, when a replacement for the Vikings of The Queen's Flight was being considered, the Air Council directed that four-engined aircraft should be selected.

The favourite contender was the Vickers Viscount, a four-engined turbine propeller aircraft in successful airline service. A study of the future role of The Queen's Flight had resulted in a requirement for an aircraft of great flexibility to provide for long-range operations with a limited passenger load or for short-range operations with a full load. Vickers Armstrong made a design study for a stretched version of the Viscount (later developed as the Viscount 400 series) but with wing-tip tanks for a transatlantic capability. This aircraft would have provided accommodation, in a single aircraft, for Royal passengers, Household staff and groundcrew. Negotiations had got to the point where Air France had graciously offered to forego a contracted airframe number so that early delivery

DH Heron C3 XH375 in flight over Windsor Castle, flown by the newly-promoted Squadron Leader Caryl Gordon, the Duke of Edinburgh's flying instructor.

The Duke of Edinburgh in the pilot's seat of his personal DH Heron C3 XH375, which replaced a Viking of The Queen's Flight in mid-1955. It was equipped to carry three crew and six passengers and had a very comprehensive radio suite. It was powered by four DH Gipsy Queen 30 Mk 2 engines with DH two-blade constant-speed airscrews.

could be made to The Queen's Flight. A life expectancy of twenty to twenty-five years was planned.

There is no doubt that if this aircraft had entered service with The Queen's Flight, it would have provided economical, safe transport, with comfort and dignity, over a wide range of the commitments. It is ironical that over ten years later the Andover was adopted, which has engines and components of Viscount lineage. Although the Andover has given excellent service for more than twenty years, it is no more than a poor man's version of the proposed Viscount.

But it was not to be; a decision was handed down that The Queen's Flight would be equipped with de Havilland Herons. The only contribution to the requirement appeared to be that it had four engines, but these were small, unsupercharged, air-cooled piston engines designed in the 1930s. A less suitable aircraft it was hard to visualise; it was probably the smallest, cheapest four-engined aircraft in existence. Sir Edward Fielden came back to Benson from London that day in one of his purple moods and disappeared into his den muttering something about 'Morris Minors instead of Daimlers'.

The four Herons supplied to The Queen's Flight (one Mk3 and three Mk4s) had a weight problem from conception; everything had to be contained within the 14,500 lbs maximum all-up weight. The aircraft had been designed as a short-range, low-altitude feeder aircraft with twelve seats, no refinements and minimal navigation and radio aids. The Queen's Flight aircraft, however, were required to operate to international airways standards, which meant having navigation and radio equipment similar to transatlantic operators. Safety requirements led to variable-pitch, fully feathering propellers being adapted to engines designed before such refinements were known. The propellers could not be unfeathered in the air for practice, as this led to engine failure from bearing-oil starvation. The weight of this extra equipment had to be paid for in reduced standards elsewhere: the toilet facilities were primitive, just a caravan-type Elsan and a wash-basin with a cold-water supply. There was no galley and

Although it was the Duke of Edinburgh's personal aeroplane, Heron XH375 was used extensively for Royal flying at home and overseas. It was in natural metal finish overall, with an Edinburgh green cheat line.

the only contribution to catering was an electric plug for a kettle, but this could only be used after first switching off the navigation aids because the total power supply was only 2Kw. Uxbridge Control took some persuading that this was a necessary technique when flying Purple Airways.

The internal layout of the Heron provided a cockpit rather than a flight-deck with tight, side-by-side seating for the pilot and navigator. The main fuselage was divided into two saloons, each with four seats. The steward or Household staff occupied the forward saloon and the Royal passengers the rear; there was only a curtain between the two saloons, the door being sacrificed to save weight. Aft of the rear saloon was a small vestibule for the entrance door and the toilet. There was no toilet in the forward part of the aircraft. As there was no galley, the stewards provided refreshments from a 'magic box' designed to fit over a seat. The box contained crockery, cutlery, glass and the food and drinks. The stewards performed wonders with these sparse facilities, even to a 'four-minute' egg being boiled in the kettle at the passengers' feet.

Externally, the aircraft was painted overall in red 'day-glow', fluorescent paint, the idea being to make it conspicuous and reduce the possibility of collision. The paint was about three times heavier than normal paint and could not be touched-up to repair minor scars. It was therefore not only a weight penalty but a financial penalty, as it cost about £10,000 per year for complete re-paint jobs. The other serious consideration was the heat absorption properties, which in the tropics resulted in The Queen enduring cabin temperatures of 120°F (measured in Ghana). There was no air-conditioning system, and ventilation by ram-air when flying only marginally reduced the temperature at low altitude. The pilot and navigator sitting under a bubble canopy while at readiness had the sympathy of onlookers.

The performance of the aircraft was poor, even in comparison with aircraft of the time. The unsupercharged engines gave it a low ceiling, so it operated in the rough weather: not a pleasant ride in a light aircraft with high aspect ratio

The Queen's Flight Herons were finished in overall fluorescent red by the end of 1961. It made the aircraft highly visible but was not popular with groundcrews, aircrews or passengers.

wings. With eight passengers it could not take a full fuel-load, which reduced the already poor range. In hot climates the weight/altitude/temperature curves were depressing: a take-off run started with the engines giving minus 2 lbs/sq in boost at take-off revs, and after 1500 yards, one hoped that the ram effect might bring it up to zero.

Servicing the aircraft was technically simple, the problems being the sheer quantity of necessary routine engine servicing and the unreliability of instrument, radio and navigation components. For instance the twin Bendix VOR equipment fitted, produced in the UK under licence, was so unreliable that despite the duplicate fit, two extra sets of black boxes were carried in the aircraft and were usually needed in the course of one day's flying. The airframe was elementary and the pneumatic system reasonably reliable, so there was not a great problem in this field. The engines, however, were a headache as they demanded frequent sparking plug changes, oil-filter changes, tuning or checking for cracked exhausts or crankcases or oil leaks: all simple, routine stuff but a burden of sheer quantity. On overseas tours, three aircraft were usually required for quite a modest party and three engineers were as many as could be carried. At the end of a day's flying it was a little daunting to have twelve dirty engines leering at you and to know that a one hundred percent turn-out was needed next day. Engineers didn't get to bed very early.

Due to the limited range and general performance, there was no question of the Herons being used to transport the Royal Family to overseas destinations. Such flights were undertaken by RAF Transport Command or British Overseas Airways. However, the Herons were used for local flying at overseas destinations, having been ferried out lightly loaded in 400-500 mile stages between fuel stops. It is surprising where those little aeroplanes got to: Vancouver, Rangoon, Dar-es-Salaam, Freetown, Accra. One notable flight was in 1961 when three aircraft were needed to fly Prince Philip and a small party from the Gambia to Dar-es-Salaam, three days across Africa with fuel stops every 400-500 miles. In some places refuelling from four-gallon tins was necessary – real Amy Johnson stuff.

It would have been better to have kept the Vikings!

THE FIRST ROYAL HELICOPTER FLIGHTS

HRH The Duke of Edinburgh had been the first member of the Royal Family to fly in a helicopter when he flew several sorties in a civil Dragonfly belonging to Westlands (G-AKTW, temporarily registered with the RAF serial number XD649 and flown by Squadron Leader Ron Gellatly) on an official visit to Germany between 18 and 20 March 1953.

The need for helicopters for Royal flights had become increasingly obvious and a visit by Princess Margaret to several Army units in Germany in July 1954 was planned to be done by helicopter within Germany. The Queen's Flight still had no helicopters of its own, so the newly-formed Central Flying School Helicopter Unit of three Dragonflies was borrowed for the occasion. In the same month, agreement in principle was given for The Queen's Flight to operate two VVIP helicopters and in September 1954, the Flight received its own first passenger-carrying helicopter – the VVIP-modified Dragonfly

HM The Queen Mother leaving Westland Dragonfly HC4 XF261 which was on loan to The Queen's Flight from the Central Flying School (Helicopter Division), South Cerney, between September 1954 and August 1958. It was the first helicopter to be permanently established as part of the Flight.

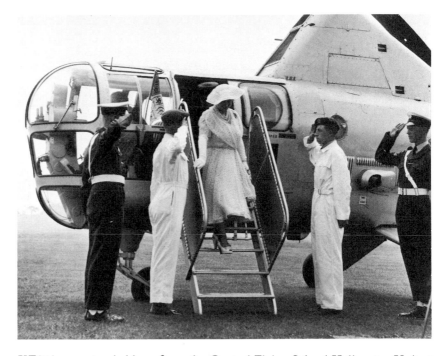

The second Westland Whirlwind HCC8, XN127, was handed over to the Commanding Officer of The Queen's Flight, Wing Commander R.G. Wakeford OBE, AFC, on 5 November 1959.

XF261, on extended loan from the Central Flying School Helicopter Unit at South Cerney. Other early users of helicopters were the Duke and Duchess of Gloucester, the Queen Mother and Princess Margaret, but it was Prince Philip who became the champion of the helicopter, soon taking a flying course and in 1955 qualifying as a helicopter pilot under the tutelage of Lieutenant-Commander M.H. Simpson, the Chief Flying Instructor of No. 705 Squadron, RN, at Gosport. Prince Philip also continued his fixed-wing flying, at first in Percival Provost WV679 and Devon VP961 and, after its delivery on 18 May 1955, in his personal de Havilland Heron C3, XH375. The latter, like the Devon, departed from the usual Queen's Flight colours in that it had an overall polished silver finish with a line along the fuselage in Edinburgh green.

As a result of administrative delays and technical problems, it was not until July 1958 that a contract for two VVIP Whirlwinds (now known as Mk 8s) was placed with Westlands, delivery being expected the following spring. A Mk 4 aircraft was collected from Aston Down at the end of the month for crew training, and the faithful Dragonfly, XF261, was returned to South Cerney in August. Air Commodore Fielden continued to press for the establishment of two helicopter crews on The Queen's Flight. He now felt that, as the Naval authorities had been so helpful with previous helicopter trips, the Admiralty should be invited to appoint a Naval helicopter pilot to join The Queen's Flight when the VVIP helicopters were delivered. Lieutenant R.M. Kerr was selected to fill this post, a post still filled by a Naval pilot. Lieutenant Kerr eventually joined the Flight in January 1960. Subsequently transferring to the RAF, he remained until 1976 as Prince Philip's personal helicopter pilot.

The Whirlwind Mk 8s received their release to service in October 1959. By this time, however, Air Commodore Fielden was showing interest in the Gnome gas-turbine powered version of the Whirlwind. The first of the new aircraft, XN126, was collected from Boscombe Down on 1 October and the second, XN127, from Yeovil on 5 November. The Mk 4 was soon disposed of, and there followed a short period of crew training and working up before the helicopters were successfully introduced to Royal flying on 23 February 1960, with a flight by the Duchess of Kent from Kensington Palace to Papworth – almost four years after the originally projected date of introduction.

The Queen's Flight's Whirlwind pilots and navigators in 1960, now including a permanent Naval pilot, Lieutenant R.M. Kerr.

PRINCE PHILIP FLIES A SINGLE-SEATER

The last Royal or Special flight in a Viking (VL247) took place on 22 April 1958 and shortly afterwards the three remaining Vikings left the Flight. They were eventually sold to Tradair. Two new Herons were collected from Hawarden on 16 April and were soon in use on special flights, XM295 making its first on 1 May and XM296 on 7 May.

On 24 October 1959, HRH The Duke of Edinburgh carried out a short flight from White Waltham in Turbulent G-APNZ. This is the only occasion on

which any member of the Royal Family has flown a single-seater aircraft. He also entered this aircraft in the National Air Races of 1959, 1960 and 1961, flown by his equerry, Squadron Leader John Severne who won the King's Cup in 1960 becoming National Air Racing Champion. Painted in Prince Philip's colours, G-APNZ was flown in the races with HRH's badge on the side. Prince Philip's interest at that time in general aviation and sporting flying gave great encouragement to the movement, particularly when, in 1959, he accepted honorary membership of the Tiger Club.

A new arrival in 1960 was a de Havilland Chipmunk T10, WP903, which was collected from Silloth in September and was painted overall fluorescent red. By this time the Herons, too, were painted fluorescent red because patches of Dayglo were appearing on many RAF aircraft as a flight safety measure. It was considered that aircraft of The Queen's Flight should be similarly treated, so the Herons lost their traditional finish of polished silver trimmed with red and blue. The basic colours were retained by the addition of a Royal blue line along the fuselage, although Prince Philip's aircraft retained its Edinburgh green line.

The Chipmunk was originally intended for use by Prince Philip but was subsequently used to teach the Duke of Kent, Prince Michael and Prince William to fly. By this time it was clear that a fourth Heron would be required to cope with the ever-increasing demand for Royal flights and, with surprisingly little discussion, it was agreed at the end of 1960 to place an order with Hawker Siddeley. To make way for the new Heron, the Devon was phased out and flown to the Maintenance Unit at Shawbury in October 1960.

The Queen's Flight continued its responsibility for the flying training of members of the Royal Family. DH Chipmunk T10 WP903, allocated to The Queen's Flight between 20 September 1962 and 12 June 1964, originally for use by Prince Philip, was also used for the instruction of the Prince of Wales, the Duke of Kent, Prince Michael and Prince William. It was finished in the overall Dayglo red paint scheme adopted by The Queen's Flight from 1961.

Before the fourth Heron could be completed, however, came the tour of India and Pakistan and the State Visit to Nepal and Iran. It was found that the Herons had insufficient carrying capacity for the mountainous regions of Nepal so the new Handley Page Herald had been suggested as the most suitable aircraft. However, the Herald was relatively untried at that time and recourse was finally made to the Dakota. Two machines were used, KN645, which had once been the personal transport of Field Marshal Lord Montgomery, and KN452, which had previously been used by the Air Officer Commanding Malta. Both aircraft were refurbished for the tour and two very experienced crews were selected to fly them, arriving at The Queen's Flight at much the same time as the new Commanding Officer, Wing Commander D.L. Attlee. The Dakotas performed well in Nepal, as did the two Heron Mk 4s which were used during the Indian and Pakistani parts of this very long tour.

The delivery of the fourth Heron on 16 June 1961 came just in time, for the existing aircraft were beginning to wilt under the volume of work: since the Indian visit, the other Mk 4 had been on tour again with the Duke of Kent to Sierra Leone. Later in the year, three Herons were on the trans-Africa flight with Prince Philip remembered earlier (page 52). On 9 July 1961, during the proving flight to West Africa for The Queen's forthcoming visit in November, Wing Commander Attlee and his crew had been arrested at Gao, in the newly independent republic of Mali (see page 146). This is thought to be the first occasion a Royal aircraft and crew had been arrested − though not, as we shall see, the last.

The record number of hours flown in 1961, 2,678.50, was not again exceeded until 1984 when a total of 2,696.10 was flown.

ANDOVERS AND WHIRLWIND MK 12S ARRIVE

On 1 January 1962, Air Commodore Sir Edward Fielden KVCO, CB, DFC, AFC, retired from The Queen's Flight and was promoted to Air Vice-Marshal and appointed Senior Air Equerry to the Queen. He was succeeded on 21 March as Captain of The Queen's Flight by Air Commodore A.D. Mitchell CVO, DFC, AFC, a previous Deputy Captain.

In May 1962, came the first mention of finding replacements for the Herons. They had given excellent service, considering their unsuitability for some of the tasks they had to perform. A working party, chaired by The Queen's Private Secretary, Sir Michael Adeane and including senior officials of the Treasury and Air Ministry, considered that another important factor weighing against the Herons was the prestige value of a large and more modern aircraft. In 1958, The Queen had been advised against using the Herons for a State Visit to the Netherlands for just that reason. After some deliberation, and consideration of the Handley Page Herald, the Hawker Siddeley HS125, HS126 and HS748 and the British Aircraft Corporation BAC 1-11, it was proposed that two of the Herons should be replaced by HS748s. It was pointed out that this move would

XS790, one of The Queen's Flight's two permanently-established Andover CC2s, photographed in December 1965 in the original finish of white upper fuselage, red wings and tail surfaces, blue cheat line and natural metal lower fuselage and engine nacelles. The Flight's Andover CC2s, XS789 and XS790, were two of the six procured by the RAF. XS794 has been lent to the Flight for short periods by the Metropolitan Communication Squadron for specific tasks.

Prince Philip in the Gnome-engined Whirlwind HCC12 XR486. The HCC12 was the VVIP version of the standard Whirlwind HAR10. Two HCC12s replaced the Flight's Whirlwind HCC8s in spring 1964.

involve little capital expenditure, since The Queen's Flight would use two of the 748s ordered by the RAF as the Andover CC Mk 2.

Replacement of the helicopters was also considered, but for the time being, work continued with the Whirlwind Mk 8s and the Herons, which in 1963 carried out tours of Cyprus and Jordan with the Duke and Duchess of Gloucester, and of Sudan.

The general RAF change-over from piston-engined Whirlwinds to the Gnome-engined HAR10 was reflected on The Queen's Flight by the arrival on 26 March 1964 of a Whirlwind HCC12, the first of the two VVIP versions of the HAR10 specially ordered for the Flight. The first Andover, XS790, was handed over to the Flight at the Hawker Siddeley Avro Division factory at Woodford on 10 July. By this time, the second HCC12 Whirlwind had arrived, the two Mk 8s being retired and eventually modified to HAR10 standard, and the Chipmunk had been returned to the MU. Air Commodore Mitchell retired on 1 August 1964, and the new Captain of The Queen's Flight, Air Commodore J.H.L. Blount DFC, took up his appointment just in time to see the re-equipment completed when, on 7 August, the second Andover arrived. For a short time, The Queen's Flight had eight aircraft on charge – two Andovers, four Herons and two Whirlwinds. This state of affairs was short-lived, however, for in September the original Heron, Prince Philip's personal Mk 3, left the Flight after nine years service and 3,560 flying hours. XM295 followed the Mk 3 in January 1965, having logged 3,710 flying hours, and the Flight settled down for the next few years with its established six aeroplanes (two Andovers, two Herons and two Whirlwinds).

With the advent of the Andovers, the remaining Herons were relegated to service within the United Kingdom and Europe. The Andovers undertook an

A typical scene at RAF Benson in the mid-1960s, with a Westland Whirlwind HCC12, a DH Heron C4 and an Andover C2. The last Heron was re-allocated in June 1968, after the type had made 941 Royal flights, flying 13,400 hours and covering two million miles.

increasing number of overseas flights during the next few years and they, the Herons and Whirlwinds were employed on a growing number of Royal and Special flights within Europe. In June 1967, the Duke and Duchess of Kent's visit to Tonga to represent The Queen at the Coronation of the King was the longest tour yet undertaken by the Flight, the aircraft flying 165 hours in five weeks.

THE WESSEX REPLACES THE WHIRLWIND

In the middle of 1967, negotiations were under way for the replacement of the Whirlwind HCC12 helicopters. The twin-engined Wessex had been in general service use for some time and a VVIP version was planned for The Queen's Flight; in fact, a standard Wessex HC2 had already been used by the Flight when XT673 was borrowed from No. 72 Squadron in July 1967 to fly Prince Philip to the North Sea oil-rig, *Sea Quest*.

In December 1967, the third Andover CC2, XS793, was ferried to Benson from Aden, where it had been used by the Commander-in-Chief. The technicians began a long period of servicing to make it ready for Royal flying because it had suffered a very heavy landing in Aden and much repair work was necessary. The Flight at the same time prepared to give up its two remaining Herons.

However, this and all other considerations were overshadowed by the tragic

XV732 and XV733, the two Westland Wessex HCC4s allocated to The Queen's Flight, were taken on charge on 25 June and 11 July 1969 respectively. They provide a very cost and time-effective means of transport for members of the Royal Family.

accident of 7 December 1967. Whirlwind XR487 was en route to Yeovil, where a meeting was to be held to discuss the VVIP Wessex, when the main rotor-shaft snapped and the helicopter crashed at Brightwalton, Berks. The accident resulted in the deaths of the crew, Squadron Leader J.H. Liversedge DFC, AFC, and Flight Lieutenant R. Fisher, and the passengers, Air Commodore J.H.L. Blount DFC, the Captain of The Queen's Flight, and Squadron Leader M.W. Hermon, the Flight's Engineering Officer. Group Captain Gordon-Cumming, one of the Deputy Captains, took over as Acting Captain of The Queen's Flight following the accident until, on 15 February 1968, Air Commodore A.L. Winskill CBE, DFC, was appointed Captain of The Queen's Flight.

All Whirlwind helicopters throughout the services were grounded pending the report of the Board of Enquiry into the accident, and The Queen's Flight did not fly another Royal helicopter sortie until the end of March 1968. A standard Whirlwind HAR10 was collected from Odiham on 31 January 1968 as a temporary replacement for the crashed HCC12, but it was not cleared for use by the Royal Family. When helicopter passenger flying was re-started, XR486 was used for all Royal flights.

On 26 May 1968, the third Andover, XS793, commenced operational flying, having been virtually rebuilt by the Flight's excellent technicians in the previous six months. This was the signal for the retirement of the Herons, and XR391, which had completed 1,820 flying hours in its seven years on the Flight, was flown to No. 27 MU at Shawbury on 17 June 1968; the last Heron Royal flight took place on 25 June 1968, and shortly afterwards XM296 was delivered to the MU at Leconfield, having completed 4,310 flying hours in its ten years of Royal service. July 1968 also saw the return to the Flight of the red-painted Chipmunk T10, WP903, which was allocated for the flying instruction of the Prince of Wales.

The first of the VVIP Wessex HCC4s was collected from Yeovil on 25 June 1969, and was in Royal use only two days later to fly the Duke and Duchess of Kent from Maidstone to Coppins. The target date for the introduction of the new helicopters had been 1 July, and the second aeroplane was handed over to Air Commodore Winskill on the appointed day. By this time, the first was operating at Caernarvon in connection with the Investiture of the Prince of Wales and his subsequent tour of the Principality. After the delivery of the Wessex, the Whirlwinds were phased out.

On 28 October 1969, Princess Anne became the first member of the Royal Family to fly in a Queen's flight helicopter to an oil-rig when she visited the *Amoco 'B'*.

THE PRINCE OF WALES GAINS HIS WINGS

In October 1969, the Prince of Wales graduated from the Chipmunk to a twin-engined trainer. A Basset CC1 was allotted in June 1969, which brought The Queen's Flight to its greatest-ever aircraft strength, briefly operating ten aircraft

The Prince of Wales made his first solo flight in Chipmunk T10 WP903 at RAF Bassingbourn on 14 January 1969.

Ab initio student pilot, the Prince of Wales, making the customary check of Chipmunk T10 WP903 before take-off, with his instructor Squadron Leader P.G. Pinney.

of six different types. The Chipmunk was eventually returned to No. 27 MU at Shawbury on 9 October 1969, having been used by the Prince of Wales for 101 flights, culminating in the award of his Private Pilot's Licence in March 1969 and his RAF Preliminary Flying Badge on 2 August 1969.

The Prince of Wales' penultimate Basset flight was on 8 March 1971 when, as an RAF Flight Lieutenant, he flew from Benson to Cranwell to join the first Graduate Entry at the RAF College and to complete his flying training under the auspices of Training Command, with over 100 hours flying in Jet Provost Mk 5s XW322 and XW323. The Prince of Wales graduated from the RAF College on 20 August 1971 and was presented with his RAF wings by the Chief of the Air Staff, Air Chief Marshal Sir Denis Spotswood.

During this time the Flight was kept busy within the United Kingdom and Europe. The helicopters in particular were worked almost to capacity in 1970, so much so that requests were made − without success − for the return of a Wessex HC2 for crew training and proving flights and to take the pressure off the HCC4s. The helicopters continued the now traditional delivery of mail to HMY *Britannia* off Western Scotland. In August 1970, whilst operating from Stornoway during this exercise, the crew of XV732 was called on to fly a doctor to the German trawler *Skagerrak*. This exploit in high seas and heavy weather earned a Queen's Commendation for the Crew Chief, Chief Technician S.A. Frost. On 14 July 1971, General Idi Amin was flown from Heathrow to Turnhouse in an Andover.

The Basset continued in use as a training aircraft for some time after the Prince of Wales had started his Cranwell course, being used to train the Duke of Kent, initially at Leuchars and later at Benson. This exercise finished in

Beagle Basset CC1 XS770 was allocated to The Queen's Flight on 27 June 1969 for the Prince of Wales' twin-engine flying instruction. After the Prince began his Cranwell course it was retained to train the Duke of Kent at Leuchars, then at Benson. It was re-allocated to No. 32 Squadron on 16 September 1971.

August 1971, and the following month the Basset was transferred to No. 32 Squadron at Northolt, leaving The Queen's Flight with the aircraft which were to serve unchanged for almost fifteen years: Andover CC2s XS789, XS790 and XS793 and Wessex HCC4s XV732 and XV733.

For some time the Andovers had shown signs of corrosion in the 'Alclad' skin of the exposed aluminium underbody, caused by continual polishing. A number of new paint schemes to solve the problem were submitted to The Queen who selected an all-white polyurethane finish for the previously natural metal areas. This was applied to XS790 in April 1971.

In May, the sad news was received that the Duke of Windsor had died. As the founder of the Prince of Wales' Flight and later, as Edward VIII, the founder of The King's Flight, it was appropriate that on 31 May 1972 his body was flown home from France to Benson, the present home of The Queen's Flight, and was laid in state in the Station Church.

Further sad news came on 28 August 1972 when HRH Prince William of Gloucester was killed when his Piper Cherokee struck a tree at the start of the Goodyear Trophy Air Race. Six Andover flights carried eleven members of the Royal Family to his funeral. Prince William had been due to visit the Middle East in September with The Queen's Flight.

THE OIL CRISIS

During 1972 and 1973, despite an unusually high turnover of engineering staff (thirty percent), the Flight had its second and third busiest years on record. The oil crisis at the end of 1973 was to have a marked effect on The Queen's Flight. However, within two years, the steady upward trend in the number of Royal flights, with both fixed and rotary wing aircraft, had been resumed. During this busy period the only change to the aircraft was the replacement of the military insignia by the Union Flag on the fins of the Andover in December 1973.

During 1973, the Megadata system was installed in the Flight Operations Room. This facility provided a direct line to airports throughout the world. For the first time, The Queen's Flight was able to operate independently of No. 38 Group for operational communications.

The effect of the oil crisis continued to cut deeply into the operations of the Flight in 1974, many trips being undertaken by civil airlines, but the Flight carried Royal visitors during 1975 to the USA, Canada, Holland, Saudi Arabia, Morocco, the Caribbean and Central American republics, Poland and Spain. Queen Elizabeth The Queen Mother toured the Channel Islands by Wessex, and also, on 14 October, made the first Royal helicopter flight on to an aircraft carrier cruising at sea: flying from her residence at Birkhall, she landed on HMS *Ark Royal* in the Moray Firth.

Although there were few overseas trips for the Andovers in 1976, all three aircraft were heavily involved in The Queen's State Visit to Luxembourg in November. One surprising aspect of Andover flying was that more hours were flown in one calendar month (237.15 in October) than ever before, beating the previous total set in November 1973.

The mail runs carried out by the Wessex to HMY *Britannia* were to cease after the hot summer of 1976 when the RN helicopter attached to *Britannia's* escort took over the task. During the year, the Wessex was re-trimmed internally and the Andover Royal Compartment was completely re-designed and refitted by the Interior Furnishings Section of the Flight. A start was made on the rationalisation of the Andover servicing schedules, the amended schedules being subsequently introduced on XS790 in June 1977.

THE SILVER JUBILEE

Her Majesty The Queen's Silver Jubilee Year, 1977, was an interesting and busy year for the Flight. The Wessex workload had been increasing by approximately ten percent a year since the fuel crisis of 1973, and Jubilee Year was to prove the busiest yet; in June and July there were seventy Royal and Special flights. For the first time, the Wessex flew in Northern Ireland, carrying the Duke of Gloucester in February, followed in March by Princess Anne's visit to the Province. The Wessex were also involved with the European Foreign Ministers' Conference at Leeds Castle in May. On 10 August, The Queen made her first helicopter flight when she flew in XV732 from HMS *Fife* (escort to the Royal Yacht) to Hillsborough Castle; she later returned to *Fife* in XV733. The next day Her Majesty flew in XV733 from *Fife* to Coleraine and returned in the same aircraft. It was fitting that both Squadron Leader J. Millar DFC and Squadron Leader R. Lee MVO, DFC, who between them had over twenty-four years service and 1,700 Royal flights, should carry the Queen on her first helicopter trip as they were due to leave the Flight in October. They received Her Majesty's Silver Jubilee Medal in June, together with forty-eight other members of the Flight.

The Andovers had an even busier year than the Wessex, with The Queen's Silver Jubilee tour of Fiji and Papua New Guinea in February, XS789 returning with Prince Philip through Afghanistan in March, having been away for eight weeks. Royal visits with the Andover were also made to Oman, Ghana, Ivory Coast, Nigeria, Canada and Jamaica. Two Andovers carrying The Queen and the Prince of Wales and a Wessex carrying the Queen Mother were involved at Finningley on 29 July for The Queen's Review of the Royal Air Force. The BAC 1-11 was at this time being considered as a replacement for the Andover and work was begun in late 1977 on revising specifications originally drawn up in 1971. This was completed in early 1978.

The rationalisation of servicing schedules successfully introduced with the Andover in 1977 was extended to the Wessex during the same year and introduced in April 1978, commencing with XV733. The Wessex tasking had continued to increase, reaching a peak in 1978, when a third navigator was posted in.

In April 1979, Prince Andrew completed his Royal Naval Pilot Grading under the auspices of The Queen's Flight in Chipmunk T10 WP904; his instructor was Lieutenant-Commander A. McK. Sinclair MBE, RN. On 30 July, the Prince of Wales took to the air in a privately-owned Tiger Moth, G-ADIA, during an informal visit to the Flight.

On 10 September 1979, following the tragic death of Lord Mountbatten and the injuries to his family in August, Lord Brabourne was airlifted from Aldergrove to Northolt, together with his family, in XS793, which was fitted for the casevac role — the first time such a role had been undertaken by The Queen's Flight.

The initial flying training of Prince Andrew was carried out by the RN Grading Flight at Benson under the auspices of The Queen's Flight. Two Chipmunk T10s were allocated for this training, together with a Naval instructor, Lieutenant-Commander Sandy Sinclair.

THE QUEEN'S FLIGHT IN THE 1980s

1980 started on a high note with the award of a Knighthood in the New Year's Honours List to the Captain of The Queen's Flight. Air Commodore Sir Archie Winskill KCVO, CBE, DFC, AE, MRAeS, received his Knighthood from The Queen at a private audience on 20 February 1980, twelve years almost to the day since he was appointed as Captain of The Queen's Flight.

Work had been resumed on the BAC 1-11 project at the end of 1979 when the concept was changed from a short to a medium-range aircraft with a special modification to increase its range to 2,400 miles. This work was completed early

The Prince of Wales carries his son, Prince William, from Andover CC2 XS789 at the end of the infant Prince's first flight, from Kemble to Aberdeen on 17 August 1982. Prince Philip also travelled on the flight, and the kangaroo and maple leaf emblems are mementoes of when his aircraft was 'zapped' by units of the RAAF and the Canadian Forces respectively. 'Zapping' is the tradition of attaching one's unit badge to a visitor's aircraft, motor car etc. Even senior officers' hats have been 'zapped'!

The decision to procure two BAe 146-100s for The Queen's Flight, following a year of evaluation in routine service, was announced in the House of Commons by Mr Geoffrey Pattie, Minister of State for Defence Procurement, on 1 August 1984. The superlative short-field performance, low noise-signature, low fuel-consumption and all-climate operability of the BAe 146 makes it a most appropriate choice. During the 1984 tour by the BAe 146-100 demonstrator, Prince Charles took the opportunity to inspect the aircraft whilst passing through Singapore. Mike Goldsmith, the civil projects director, and Peter Sedgwick, the deputy chief test pilot, showed him the interior, while John Loader (left), the 146 general sales manager, and Bob Hornall (right), the demonstration tour manager, accompanied him on his inspection of the airframe.

in 1980 and in April, Prince Philip made a series of flights from Benson in a BAC 1-11 of British Aerospace, G-ASYD.

The Prince of Wales made an informal visit to the Flight in March, in the course of which he was presented by the Captain with a memento to commemorate His Royal Highness's 1,000 flying hours. Prince Edward, following in his brother's footsteps, took to the air at Benson and attained his Gliding Proficiency Certificate in July in a Sedburgh Glider XN151.

On 27 March 1981, shortly after the engagement of the Prince of Wales to Lady Diana Spencer was announced, Lady Diana made her first journey with the Flight in a Wessex, accompanying the Prince of Wales to Cheltenham.

The flying commitment built up steadily during 1981, and April, June and September were the busiest-ever respective months. On 2 June, all five aircraft of the Flight flew on task and achieved fourteen Royal flights in one day, which is believed to be a record.

The wedding of the Prince of Wales and Lady Diana Spencer took place on 29 July 1981. Twelve members of the Flight were privileged to attend the wedding, to act as ushers and to form part of the step-lining contingent at Westminster Abbey. On 1 August, the Prince and Princess were flown from Southampton to Gibraltar on their honeymoon by Squadron Leader D. Lovett on what was his last flight in the Royal Air Force after nine years on the Flight.

The year ended on a sad note when the Captain, Sir Archie Winskill, made his last flight before retirement. His tenure of office of almost fourteen years was exceeded only by Sir Edward Fielden. He was succeeded on 27 January 1982 by Air Vice-Marshal J. de M. Severne LVO, OBE, AFC, a former Equerry to the Duke of Edinburgh.

On 25 June 1982, the Prince of Wales became the first member of the Royal Family to make a helicopter flight from British to foreign soil when he flew to Port Antifer, France. Then, on 11 July, he flew a Wessex on to SS *Canberra* in Southampton Water to welcome home returning servicemen from the Falklands. On 17 September, The Queen flew from Lee-on-Solent to Aberdeen in an Andover after welcoming home Prince Andrew in HMS *Invincible*. A number of other sorties were flown throughout the summer with the Royal Family to meet the homecoming ships and aircraft of the Task Force.

During 1982, the modification programme to fit a dual radio-compass system to the Andover and the two-year programme to refurbish the Andover flight-deck were completed. The Wessex cockpit had been similarly refurbished in 1981. During August, a revised Andover servicing was introduced, the basic servicing periodicity being changed from a flying to a calendar base. British Aerospace/Teleflex Morse presented the Flight with improved first pilot and co-pilot seats for the Andover.

Shortly after the cessation of hostilities in the Lebanon in 1982, Princess Anne, as President of the UK Save the Children Fund, visited Beirut while returning from her tour of Southern and East Africa at the end of the year. On a proving flight during this tour, Squadron Leader G.H. Laurie, his crew and

This artist's impression of BAe 146 ZE700 in The Queen's Flight's colours reveals differences from the pattern eventually approved. In late 1985, the red vertical tail became a smarter white, while the blue fuselage cheat line was moved down to be more visible from below. The type was well-proven in airline service when the executive version was ordered for The Queen's Flight, and it was thoroughly evaluated by the RAF, including intensive cold-weather trials in Canada. This high-lift, short-haul airliner was first flown on 3 September 1981. Orders were swiftly fulfilled for UK, US, African, Australian and Brazilian airlines, confirming claims that it set new standards. Optimised for multi-sector routes over 150 miles, it is capable of ranges up to 1,500 miles. Two versions are offered: the 146-100, seating 71-93 passengers, and the 111-passenger 146-200 with a longer cabin. The Queen's Flight aircraft are standard 146-100 airframes with luxury cabins and wing-root fuel tanks to extend ranges up to 1,700 miles. The two-crew operation flight deck has exceptional visibility. A Smiths SEP-10 autopilot is fitted. The high-lift wing section, which allows a steep climb-out after take-off and a low-speed approach, makes complicated leading-edge flaps and slats and engine thrust reversers unnecessary. The four 6,970 lb-thrust Avco Lycoming ALF 502R-5 turbofans give exemplary fuel economy at cruising altitudes and combine with the wing to provide excellent short-field performance. The engine's high bypass ratio of 5.9:1 and the highly efficient wing produce a particularly quiet aeroplane.

aircraft were held on the ground by Zimbabwean troops at Aberdeen Two for some two hours on 18 October 1982, in circumstances remarkably similar to Wing Commander Attlee's incident twenty-one years earlier in Mali.

1982 was very satisfactorily rounded off on 22 December when Mr John Nott, the Secretary of State for Defence, announced in the House that the RAF would purchase two BAe 146s in the spring of 1983. Subject to a satisfactory two-year proving period, The Queen's Flight would subsequently re-equip with the extended-range version of the aircraft.

HRH Prince William had flown for the first time on 17 August 1982, from Kemble to Aberdeen with his parents and Prince Philip. On 4 March 1983 he travelled on his first journey as a principal passenger with the Flight when his parents disembarked at Glasgow to fulfil public engagements and the infant Prince travelled on to Aberdeen. His brother, Prince Henry, first flew when he accompanied his parents from Northolt to Aberdeen on 22 March 1985.

The use of The Queen's Flight's helicopters has continually increased: when

XV732 reached 5,000 flying hours on 15 March 1983, it raised to over 10,000 the total hours flown by the two Wessex since their introduction to the Flight in 1969. Further milestones were attained when Andover XS789 reached a total of 10,000 hours on 24 May, the same total being achieved by XS790 five days later.

1984 arrived with the confirmation that the evaluation of the BAe 146 at Brize Norton had been successful and that The Queen's Flight was to be re-equipped with two BAe 146 aircraft in 1986. It was also confirmed that, due to the present and projected tasking, one Andover would remain to maintain a total of three fixed-wing aircraft. The first 146 for the Flight, ZE700, entered the production track at Hatfield on 30 January, followed by ZE701, on 9 June. ZE700 made its maiden flight on 23 November, to Hawarden, where it remained for completion of the interior fit. The 146 contract was signed on 27 November 1984.

Princess Anne for the first time became the most prolific user of the Flight, including in 1984 strenuous tours of West Africa and the Indian sub-continent in her capacity as President of the Save the Children Fund. Princess Anne's tour of India was cut short due to the assassination of Mrs Gandhi whilst the Andover was at Delhi.

During 1985 the Flight carried members of the Royal Family on a record number of 856 occasions. As the new chapter represented by the BAe 146s opened, the Flight could look back over fifty years of achievement and service, but also looked forward with determination to maintain what are probably the most exacting standards of any flying unit in the world.

3

THE CAPTAIN OF
THE QUEEN'S FLIGHT

The title 'Captain of The Queen's Flight' can be traced back to the *London Gazette* of 20 July 1936 which stated, inter alia: 'The King has been graciously pleased to make the following appointments to His Majesty's Household, to date from the 21st July 1936: Flight Lieutenant Edward Hedley Fielden, AFC, Captain of The King's Flight.'

'Mouse' Fielden, as he was known to all his friends, was the only pilot of the one and only aircraft of The King's Flight, and therefore 'Captain' accurately described his role. Now, with about twenty-two officers and one hundred and sixty airmen of many trades, together with three civilians, in The Queen's Flight, the Captain no longer flies the aircraft, but he is in overall command of The Queen's Flight and is responsible for all aspects of its operation.

When The King's Flight was re-formed after the war, the Flight carried out about 130 Royal flights a year, but since the introduction of helicopters in the mid-1950s there has been a steady increase until we are now flying over five times that number of flights annually with the same number of aircraft. Many of the flights are overseas and require a considerable degree of planning and research; the Captain therefore has two deputies, both serving Group Captains, to assist him in this task.

In addition to being responsible for everything that happens on the Flight, the Captain is required to advise The Queen and members of the Royal Family on all aspects of aviation; this ranges from planning the air travel arrangements for a major State Visit overseas by The Queen, involving up to fifty passengers and eight tons of baggage, to arranging a parachute jump or a flight in a glider for one of the young Princes. The work is thus very varied and demands a broad practical knowledge of all aspects of flying.

(Text continues on page 73)

*A young Edward H. Fielden
photographed in the full dress
of a Royal Air Force Flight
Lieutenant. Fielden was the
first Captain of The King's
Flight and his character has
left an indelible mark on the
traditions of the Flight.*

*The Duke of Edinburgh's
Equerry, Squadron Leader
John Severne, swings the
propeller of Rollason
Turbulent G-APNZ at White
Waltham on 24 October 1959.
Air Vice-Marshal Severne is
the present Captain of The
Queen's Flight.*

During an informal visit by HRH The Prince of Wales to The Queen's Flight in March 1980, the then Captain, Air Commodore Sir Archie Winskill KCVO, CBE, DFC, AE, MRAeS, presented him with a memento to commemorate His Royal Highness's 1000 flying hours. The Captain had received his knighthood from the Queen a few weeks earlier on 20 February, almost exactly twelve years after taking up the post.

The Royal New Zealand Air Force has provided members of the Royal Family on tour with pristine aircraft on several occasions.

The Queen arriving in a Cosmopolitan of the Canadian Forces. Canada, New Zealand and Australia are normally the only countries in which The Queen will fly in an aircraft other than those of The Queen's Flight, British Airways or British Caledonian. The Captain of The Queen's Flight has a duty to advise The Queen on the suitability of any aircraft in which she or any member of the Royal Family wishes to fly.

The Royal Australian Air Force often conveys Royal passengers. The aircraft is a Boeing 707.

Special engineering rules have been laid down by all three services for the preparation of military aircraft for flights by members of the Royal Family. These rules are designed not only to add that little bit of extra safety to the exercise, but also to ensure, as far as possible, that the aircraft will be one hundred per cent serviceable on the day. It is not feasible, therefore, for a member of the Royal Family to fly at very short notice in a military aircraft because it would not have been possible to carry out the necessary checks and to prepare that aircraft in the limited time available. Of course, aircraft of The Queen's Flight are maintained at all times to these exacting standards and very short-notice Royal flights in our aircraft are occasionally carried out.

When the Queen flies overseas for a State Visit, the aircraft of The Queen's

Flight are not big enough to take the load, so an aircraft is usually chartered from British Airways for the task. If flying to Australia, Canada or New Zealand, Her Majesty will probably be offered an aircraft from their Air Force or national airline; indeed, pilots and crews from those Commonwealth countries have rendered notable service in flying members of the Royal Family many thousands of miles safely and comfortably. However, the Captain of The Queen's Flight will have been closely involved with the planning for all such flights and will still accompany The Queen, even though the aircraft does not belong to The Queen's Flight.

In other countries it is a well-established procedure that The Queen will only fly in aircraft of The Queen's Flight (except that in the USA, the President has on occasions invited her to make use of Air Force One). If, then, Her Majesty flies overseas in an aircraft of British Airways and wishes subsequently to fly to an airfield which is too small for that aircraft to use, The Queen's Flight will pre-position its own BAe 146 or Andover for that particular exercise. Both aircraft have exceptionally good short-field performances and are well used to flying into remote airfields all over the world.

The Captain is an Extra Equerry to Her Majesty The Queen and is the only member of the Flight who is a member of the Royal Household. As such he is in constant touch with the Private Secretaries of those members of the Royal Family who fly with the Flight. He is responsible to the Chief of the Air Staff for the safe and efficient operation of The Queen's Flight and he is therefore in close touch with the Ministry of Defence, HQ Strike Command and HQ No. 1 Group to ensure that the Flight is able to meet its tasks as effectively as possible.

The Captain always accompanies The Queen and the Queen Mother whenever they fly anywhere in the world, and when he or his deputies accompany members of the Royal Family in the air they are known as 'The Commodore'. The Commodore will liaise between the Royal Household and the aircraft crew during the planning stages and also on the day itself to ensure that everything runs as smoothly as possible. When flying with organisations which are not used to flying the Royal Family, such as British Airways or a Commonwealth Air Force, it is a comfort for the crew to feel that they have someone to turn to if they have any problems; similarly, it is helpful to the Household to know that they have a familiar face on board if they have any queries concerning the flight. 'Mouse' Fielden introduced this system long after he ceased being the pilot and it has proved its worth time and time again.

Life is never dull on The Queen's Flight! Indeed, I can honestly say that it is the most interesting and rewarding appointment I have ever held.

4

THE COMMANDING OFFICER

'Mike, the Director wants to see you,' came the summons from my Wing Commander to report to the Director of Personnel (Air).

At the time I was working as a desk officer within the Air Secretary's Department, responsible for the postings and appointments of junior officers within Support Command. What on earth could the Director want of me? Who had I posted that I shouldn't have, or worse still, which Station Commander was short of flying instructors?

Grasping my various manning charts and briefing notes, I set off for the Director's office, to be greeted with a warm smile from the secretary. 'Can't be too bad, then,' I thought, and was ushered straight in to see Air Commodore P.P.W. Taylor, the Director.

'Ah, Mike. As you know, the Promotion Board have just finished their deliberations and I'm pleased to tell you that subject to interview with the Captain of The Queen's Flight, you are to be promoted and appointed as Officer Commanding The Queen's Flight.'

'That's marvellous news. Thank you very much indeed, sir'.

Few aircrew officers enjoy flying a mahogany bomber, and I was no exception. Promotion had brought me an early release from my ground appointment and the chance to return to flying; in this instance in command of the finest flying unit in the world.

With only a limited period of time before my predecessor was to retire, there was a flurry of activity to find my own replacement and then a hurried conversion course on the Andover before finally joining The Queen's Flight, where I was to continue my apprenticeship for three months before eventually taking command.

My handover brief started with an explanation of the organisation of the

Flight. It was explained to me that the Captain was in ultimate command and, with the assistance of two Deputy Captains, he made all the detailed travel arrangements with the various Royal households. Then as CO, it was my responsibility to ensure that the aircraft were available to meet the tasks and that the Flight was correctly administered. The analogy given to explain the division of responsibilities was that the Captain could be likened to the travel agent who deals directly with a customer and makes the reservations, whereas the CO is responsible for running the airline which then takes the customer on his or her journey.

In the case of The Queen's Flight, the airline consists of three Andover fixed-wing aircraft and two Wessex helicopters and around 185 men of all ranks. To

One of the satisfactions for the Commanding Officer lies in seeing the personnel of The Queen's Flight consistently achieving the very highest standards possible for a flying unit.

An Andover of The Queen's Flight carrying HM The Queen and flown by the Flight's CO, Wing Commander Mike Schofield, taxies in at Trinidad against a dramatic cloud-drop during the 1985 Commonwealth Conference tour in the West Indies.

fly the Andovers there are four crews, the CO being captain of one, and there are three crews for the Wessex. As both Prince Philip and the Prince of Wales fly the Andover and Wessex whenever possible, one of the crews on each aircraft type is designated as the personal crew to each Prince and, as far as is possible, will always fly with him to provide an element of continuity.

To support the flying task, the Flight has its own dedicated engineering, administrative, operations, security and helicopter support staffs, relying on RAF Benson – our home station – only for accounting, medical and accommodation services. In a way, The Queen's Flight is a 'mini' RAF station within a station, and as CO my duties range far and wide, from dealing with the selection of officers to join the Flight, to welfare and discipline problems (few), to discussing aircraft servicing programmes with my Senior Engineering Officer. As mentioned earlier, I also serve as one of the Andover pilots and usually fly as the Captain of the aircraft carrying either HM The Queen or HM The Queen Mother.

Whilst the sheer variety of responsibilities, coupled with varied and interesting flying, provides me with all the job satisfaction I could wish for, the greatest satisfaction comes from seeing the standards which are achieved by all the men who support the flying task, and who in fact are The Queen's Flight. The achievement of the highest standards becomes apparent on first entering The Queen's Flight's hangar and seeing the highly polished floor on which stand the equally immaculate aircraft, which must be the best maintained in the world. I still stop and stare in admiration each time I walk into the hangar.

Apart from periods of planned servicing which take a known time to complete, an aircraft will be considered to be available for tasking, and in the event of an unserviceability will always be brought back to a fully serviceable state at the earliest opportunity. This occasionally gives rise to some nail-biting when an aircraft returns to base with an unserviceability and is required to fly again the following day. It is at such times that the existence of The Queen's Flight's unique and autonomous support facilities prove their worth: our own

The personal flag flown on the aircraft carrying The Queen, which is usually captained by the Officer Commanding The Queen's Flight. This flag is used only in Commonwealth countries which are not monarchies. In all other countries, one of Her Majesty's personal standards is flown.

technical staff can diagnose the problem or liaise directly with a manufacturer with whom they will have been able to establish a rapport over the years; our supply specialist can make the arrangements to obtain and transport whatever spares are required; and our own vehicles and drivers can be despatched to collect the items. In the meantime, work will continue around the clock until the aircraft is again fully serviceable, placing great demands on our airmen and their families, who all have to endure the large amounts of 'overtime' incurred.

Perhaps strangely, aircraft serviceability and availability are the least of my concerns; if my engineers say that an aircraft will be available, then it will be. This dedication and loyalty, coupled with a pride in work and pursuit of excellence, are characteristics which are displayed in all areas of our operation, it is something in which any CO would be able to take great pride, and I am no exception. But then every man on The Queen's Flight feels that way, too.

5

AN OVERSEAS TOUR

'Mbeya Tower, this is Kittyhawk Four. Field in sight, landing at 0756 for doors open on the hour, will call downwind righthand for runway 13'. The end of the first 'Royal' sector is almost upon us, the culmination of six months' work involving The Queen's Flight, HRH The Princess Anne's Household, British Embassies and High Commissions, the Save the Children Fund and the various host Governments, to name but a few. The provision of air transport for overseas Royal Tours is an important role for The Queen's Flight. This particular tour, carried out by Princess Anne in November-December 1985 was to Tanzania, Mozambique, Zambia and Sudan. It comprised a large number of official engagements on behalf of the Foreign and Commonwealth Office but also included visits to projects run by the Save the Children Fund of which Her Royal Highness is President. In many cases the Andover landed at airfields and strips not normally served by even internal airline services.

We are often asked why our Andovers go these vast distances to fly members of the Royal Family and why local pilots who know the area are not used. All Royal flying revolves round safety, engineering, security and quality of catering as well as the basic flying operations. For many it is hard to understand how a crew fresh from UK can be more suitable than the local crews. We have normally seen the airfield before during a proving flight (in this case made in October 1985), or on a previous tour. A crew used to operating with each other and used to the Royal flying environment will have no hesitation in diverting if conditions dictate. Certainly there will be no 'pressing on beyond reasonable grounds', whereas an operator who knows the area backwards may continue; the annual accident summaries continue to have far too many reports bearing this out!

VISIT BY HRH
THE PRINCESS ANNE
TO AFRICA

19 NOVEMBER – 8 DECEMBER 1985

———— ROYAL FLIGHTS

– – – – POSITIONING FLIGHTS

EGYPT

SUDAN

KHARTOUM

ZALINGEI

NYALA

GEDAREF

DJIBOUTI

ETHIOPIA

SOMALIA

KENYA

MOGADISHU

LAKE MANYARA

TANZANIA

MBEYA

MOMBASA

ZANZIBAR

DAR-ES-SALAAM

MWINILUNGA

MFUWE

SONGEA

KASOMPE

ZAMBIA

LUSAKA

CHIPATA

MOZAMBIQUE

QUELIMANE

INHAMBANE

MAPUTO

The planning of this tour began with a dialogue of signals between the British Embassies and High Commissions with the office of HRH The Princess Anne, with suggested programmes to be followed in the various host countries. The Queen's Flight is often asked for the nearest suitable airfield or strip to a particular place. We check maps, Aerad and Jeppesen Flight Guides and we also check with No 1 AIDU (RAF Northolt) who store the Air Information Publications (AIP/Air Pilots) of most countries in the world and with the British Embassy or High Commission concerned. In many cases we never hear of that particular place again. Slowly, however, a draft programme evolves.

In this case our own proving flight (in XS793) was to be combined with the recce to be done by the Royal Household. Whilst the Private Secretary and Personal Protection Officer visited the various sites to be visited by HRH, the crew checked the airfields, fire cover, air traffic facilities, refuelling installations, in-flight catering kitchens and airport security. At the planning stage of this tour, it was clear that at many of the destinations fire cover and air traffic facilities would have to be found from outside. We were also getting some conflicting reports on the state of various strips in Sudan. The rainy season had only just finished and the situation was changing daily. Some of the strips would have to be visited by light aircraft before taking the Andover in, even on the prover. We also had the added complication that at the end of the proving flight, the aircraft was required at Nairobi to complete a Royal task with HRH Prince Philip, so we could not afford any damage on a strip on our proving flight.

Back at Benson, the plan for the proving flight and the draft programme for the Royal tour were studied by the crew. The performance manuals were used to work out our take-off performance – somewhat limited on 1000-metre strips in temperatures expected to be ISA + 20. In some instances fuel would need to

Andover XS789 being prepared for departure at Lake Manyara, Tanzania. The strip was 1200 metres long and 4150 feet above sea level. Because of the field-length limitations, the Andover routed via Kilimanjaro International to take on fuel before continuing to Dar-es-Salaam. Princess Anne had driven 1½ hours from the Ngorongoro Crater.

Princess Anne arriving at Mwinilunga in North-Western Province of Zambia. After being greeted by political officials, Her Royal Highness was greeted by local dancers in national dress. She then drove for two hours on unmade roads to visit the Kalene Mission Hospital.

Refuelling the hard way at Kasompe, in the Copperbelt Province of Zambia. Each 45-gallon drum is checked and then pumped in for ten minutes! The photograph shows BP (Zambia) staff from nearby Ndola pumping, whilst an engineer from The Queen's Flight works on the wing of the Andover.

be positioned especially for us. Were the logistics to do this feasible? We re-checked our planning to ensure that the positioning of fuel really was essential for the task to be completed. Unfortunately, on this tour, it most certainly was! We also had to guarantee supplies of water methanol which is used in the Rolls-Royce Dart engine to restore power in both hot and high-altitude conditions. Again the schedule was checked to see if this also needed to be positioned. We had already heard that Mozambique had none in the country and supplies could not be guaranteed even if specifically ordered.

The Save the Children Fund operated a Cessna 210 (G-BFLC) in Sudan and this was to prove invaluable during the proving flight. We were able to visit two of the most limiting strips in this light aircraft prior to committing the Andover. As it transpired, all the strips in Sudan, although far from ideal, were suitable for the limited operation we required.

In Tanzania it was another story; the strip at Lake Manyara near the Ngorongoro Crater was marginal in length, so again it was visited by light

The aircraft Captain helps one of The Queen's Flight's engineers to top up with water methanol prior to departure from Nyala in the Darfur region of West Sudan. The proof of the 1½ hours spent polishing can be well seen.

aircraft first. Although the approaches were satisfactory, the first third of the runway had too many loose stones to be safe. However, the captain and navigator were assured that labour would be provided for a working party to do whatever we considered necessary. We therefore agreed that with the work completed, we would land the Andover at Lake Manyara on the Royal tour. Fire cover would drive the 3½ hours from Kilimanjaro International Airport. We also arranged for an expatriate pilot to fly his light aircraft in to act as Air Traffic Control and to confirm that the work requested had been carried out.

At Songea, also in Tanzania, we learnt that the refuelling would be from 45-gallon drums as there was no bowser. This in itself does not present a problem, except that a short stop-over was planned and it could take between two and three hours to hand-pump the fuel into our tanks. Luckily, in this case the programme was amended to give us an overnight stop.

Mozambique presented us with few problems, as we were operating from tarmac runways throughout. So we thought! However, on arrival at Quelimane

we had considerable difficulty getting fuel supplied. Eventually we had to get authority from the Regional Governor, and we were made only too aware that the war in the north of Mozambique is still a reality. We were the first aircraft of The Queen's Flight to visit Mozambique, but in spite of this initial setback, the overall impression was one of friendliness and a keenness to help.

Our final point of call on the proving flight was to Zambia, where two of the five destinations had been visited eighteen months previously with HRH The Prince of Wales. More over-wing refuelling from drums at Mfuwe, but again it transpired that the Royal party required a night-stop. The aircraft was then duly handed over to its new crew in Nairobi for their visit with Prince Philip to Madagascar, whilst we flew back to the UK by RAF VC-10 for just thirteen days prior to picking up XS789 for the Royal Tour.

The aircraft of The Queen's Flight are on the Military Register, which means we have to apply for diplomatic clearance to overfly or land in every country on our route. The workload of the signals alone for the navigator is considerable. The route, point of entry and exit from each country, together with the time, have to be quoted. Some of the clearances only come through a matter of forty-eight hours before they are required. Our Operations staff collate the replies and the clearance numbers, which have to be quoted on the flight plans. Luckily, this time most came through speedily, and when we left UK, only Mozambique

The view from the flight-deck of Andover XS789 at 100 feet on the final approach to Zalingei in the Darfur region of West Sudan. The strip, a mixture of sand and grass, is just under 1200 metres in length and 3000 feet above sea level. Note the guards on horseback alongside the main road!

86

and Sudan were outstanding; as they were both receiving the Royal visitor, we did not anticipate any problems.

So it was 12 November when we departed Benson. The crew consisted of captain, co-pilot, navigator, crew chief, steward and policeman (our basic crew) plus three engineers to give us adequate trade cover to keep the aircraft running for a month and over a hundred hours flying. The Royal programme was confirmed, fuel in position, catering orders confirmed, the availability of bottled water checked as in many places the local water was suspect. Certainly it was essential for the crew to take great care, in order to stay fit for the four-week trip. The co-pilot had collected the 'imprest', in this case considerable sums in Sterling and US dollars, to pay our bills around the route. The Queen's Flight or not, cash in hand and an American Express card say far more than 'Our Embassy will pay'! Throughout the trip, much of the co-pilot's time away from the aircraft will be spent settling hotel bills, aircraft handling bills and the like.

We soon reached Dar-es-Salaam in Tanzania, where we were to meet up with the Royal party. On our arrival the first check is 'Are there any changes to my published programme?' This must be followed by a check of the host country's own programme and any anomalies discussed. Luckily this tour was remarkably clear from such problems.

Our real job had begun: to get HRH from place to place safely, comfortably (not always easy in the heat of midday in Africa) and on time. The navigator has declared his 'doors time' some months previously; now the team has to make it. We rely on the Royal party running to time and in this we are lucky that they do

Andover XS789 departing the strip at Zalingei in Darfur, West Sudan, in a cloud of sand. Princess Anne had driven 4½ hours on unmade roads from the Save The Children Fund camp at Umbala. An SCF Partenavia P68C (G-OJCT), recently delivered from the UK, is seen in the background.

their job in such a professional manner that they are normally at the aircraft very close to the appointed time. It is easy to lose time in the Andover but very difficult to make it up. We try to find out early on in the exercise which runway will be in use at our destination, as this will often vary taxy times, so our planned touch-down time needs to be adjusted. We can fine tune at the last minute but must avoid an obviously slow taxy and even worse, the opposite! Once on the ground it is simply a matter of taxying to the agreed spot and shutting down on time, so that the rear door can be opened to the second! This always assumes that we are parking where it was agreed on the proving flight and that the red carpet is rolled to the back door. This is hard to get through to many people, as all first class airline passengers alight at the front. Again, this tour proved successful in this respect.

Whilst the Royal passenger is away from the aircraft, the crew clean the inside and outside of the aircraft before anything else is considered. The overall cleanliness of the aircraft is always commented upon, but cleaning 'a little and often' is essential for it to stay that way. The worst surface to operate from is the 'murram', a red natural surface found in many parts of Africa; the dust gets everywhere. We often chat to the inevitable crowds who have gathered to watch five or six Englishmen polish an aircraft in the heat of the noonday sun!

We also visit the fire-crew. At one destination, the local airport fire officer proudly showed us his Land-Rover and fire trailer which, he announced, had been made in England in 1839. The plate he pointed out on the side did indeed say 1839 – manufacturers since 1839. We could not spoil his image of British reliability. We had a report of the fire engine at an airfield not far away that had appeared in the original draft programme. The fire engine there is pushed out

British Airways flight number 152 departs Khartoum for Cairo and London with HRH Princess Anne at the completion of her 23-day, four-country tour of Africa. The aircraft, seen here from the cockpit of the Andover as it awaited departure clearance for Cairo, was a Tristar 200 (G-BEAK). Her Royal Highness will arrive back in the UK two days quicker than if she had made the journey by Andover!

at the start of flying and pushed back at the end of the day. The pushing is necessary as the engine was taken out for repair some months previously! This would be bad enough but worse − it does not contain any water. The reason is simple enough from the locals' viewpoint: it is too heavy to push when full!

The tour is a gruelling one, and HRH The Princess Anne works a full day from the start on 18 November until 9 December, when the tour finishes in Khartoum. Our input works well, the aircraft remains serviceable, and the only slight 'hiccup' is an enforced overshoot at Gedaref in Sudan: a vehicle bringing a young girl to present a bouquet to HRH drove past a guard and onto the strip as the Andover was on approach. We landed successfully at the second attempt. The explanation was simple − the guard was a Private, the driver a Captain. At least Lieutenant-Colonel Peter Gibbs (Private Secretary to HRH The Princess Anne) could understand that one.

So it was 8 December when the twin flags flew for the last time on the Andover (HRH's personal standard on the left, the host nation on the right) as we completed our involvement in this tour, except, that is, to fly home a number of gifts presented to HRH by the four countries concerned.

Behind every successful tour is a dedicated team. Not just the engineers down the route, but the Operations staff and engineers at base, and the MT drivers ready to rush spares to Heathrow should we need them. In this case we were lucky, since the aircraft stayed one hundred per cent serviceable within our existing route spares. The General Office staff prepare all the visa applications; the signals staff at RAF Benson send out our diplomatic clearance requests; the staff at our Embassies and High Commissions see to all our needs and liaise with the respective foreign governments. And when we return, the Accounts staff have to check all the bills we have paid, over ninety per cent of which are in US dollars as most countries insist on visitors settling accounts in hard currency. Hundreds of people outside, as well as the entire strength of The Queen's Flight, work together to produce the end result − a tour fit for a Princess.

6

THE QUEEN'S FLIGHT ENGINEERS

The Queen's Flight engineers have a straightforward task. This is to provide three one hundred per cent serviceable Andovers and two one hundred per cent serviceable Wessex in immaculate condition to meet about 800 Royal flights a year and to ensure that whenever they fly, they can not only be operated with maximum safety but also depart and arrive within five seconds of their planned time. This task is unique, and it is interesting to compare the challenge that it brings with the requirements of a typical small airline.

Although most airlines fly more hours per day on each aircraft they can, and routinely do, fly with various parts unserviceable. The aircraft are designed to allow this to be done to give the airline some flexibility to repair the inevitable unserviceabilities at the least inconvenient time. The Queen's Flight never despatches an aircraft from base with even the least important system inoperative, because we need to ensure the maximum probability of completing each task.

Most airlines fly largely back and forth between a limited range of airports, most of which have the airline's own maintenance facilities. The Queen's Flight aircraft often spend weeks away, operating from small, remote airfields in far-flung continents.

Provided a commercial airliner is reasonably clean and tidy, it is acceptable for airline use. The Queen's Flight aircraft are constantly in the public eye and need to be fit for a queen inside and out, so they are always kept in immaculate condition.

Most airlines consider they are doing well to despatch ninety-seven per cent of their aircraft within fifteen minutes of the scheduled time. The Queen's Flight achieves 99.95 per cent despatch reliability within our five-second target. We try to achieve one hundred per cent but when operating a complex machine

The port Rolls-Royce Dart turbo-prop of one of The Queen's Flight's Andovers undergoing routine maintenance. The Flight's technicians are among the finest in the Royal Air Force, and the standards laid down and consistently met are among the most exacting. They are considerably assisted in their task by the proven reliability and ease of maintenance of both the Dart and the Andover airframe, which is based on the familiar commercial HSA 748.

such as an aircraft, this is almost impossible – we know this best from those occasions when we almost do not make it!

As an example, an Andover recently had electrical generator problems on the way into Leeds airport while taking a Royal passenger to visit the city. Once the passengers had departed, the Crew Chief diagnosed a faulty voltage regulator but did not have a replacement in the small on-board spares package. A call back to base rapidly had a spare part and an electrician and tool-kit ready to go, but we only had about three hours to the planned departure time with the Royal passenger. Leeds was too far to get there in time by road but luckily one of our Wessex was available. The normal flight time by Wessex is ninety minutes and, allowing for the time to change the regulator and check the system on a ground run, it would be a close call. The hangar team rapidly prepared the Wessex and it was despatched with the rescue team within fifteen minutes of the call for help. Luck was with us, as very strong southerly winds gave the Wessex a much higher than normal groundspeed. The job was done with about ten minutes to spare and the Royal passenger knew nothing of the drama needed to achieve his

Looking like a cross between an awkward Christmas present and a very shocked caterpillar, one of the Wessex undergoes a re-spray. Since The Queen's Flight's fixed and rotary-wing aircraft are so constantly in the public eye, it is essential to ensure they are truly 'fit for a Queen'.

planned departure. Since then we have had other problems with these voltage regulators and now there is one in every on-board spares package.

This is the sort of activity that can go into achieving our almost one hundred per cent despatch reliability. Of course, when overseas, a similar occurrence in Trinidad, Khartoum or Bombay or any of the hundreds of even less accessible places we visit would be a different matter. For that reason, each aircraft on tour carries a much wider range of spare parts and a team of four engineers to keep it in perfect order. Re-supply facilities are also arranged via commercial or military airfreight to replace any parts used. Technical support and spare parts can be on their way immediately in response to a call from the aircraft on HF radio from anywhere in the world, at any time of day or night.

Arrangements to airfreight parts are made by our small supply section, which for very good reasons is a fully integrated part of the engineering organisation. Many of the aircraft's critical parts are subject to additional quality assurance procedures during manufacture or overhaul to enhance their safety and reliability. Where a similar item, such as a Wessex main rotor gearbox, is also in the rest of the MOD inventory, ours are specifically identified and closely controlled by our supply section. Even the transport of such equipments to and from repair at the manufacturers is done with our own vehicles and drivers. For additional safety and reliability, most components are removed and serviced more often than those on the equivalent military aircraft. The servicing work carried out within the confines of our one hangar at Benson is greater in scope than that on any other unit in the RAF.

It is unusual to have the combination of both helicopters and fixed-wing aircraft on the same unit. It is also very rare to find the same group of engineers both handling aircraft on daily flying operations and carrying out complete overhauls, often lasting several months, on the same machines. Our engineers have the unique opportunity to exercise their skills in both these areas and also to work in our workshops stripping and repairing components such as engines, gearboxes and electrical and avionic black boxes removed from the aircraft. This broad field of employment gives immense job satisfaction and requires the very best tradesmen, who must have a total commitment to their work.

Each year we undertake at least five large scheduled servicings, one on each aircraft. The shortest of these takes four weeks, and careful long-range planning is needed to ensure that only one Wessex or Andover is serviced at any time. In the 1950s, aircraft utilisation was low, but since then there has been at least a five-fold increase in tasking and we rarely have the luxury of a reserve aircraft. We maintain a rigid policy of working on every returning aircraft until it is completely serviceable, regardless of the time of day or night or of the effort involved.

The aircraft typically leave Benson early in the morning and return in late afternoon or early evening. Most engineering work is therefore done overnight. Even the smallest defects are always fully investigated and repaired immediately

This crowded scene in the hangar at RAF Benson, with Wessex XV732 and XV733, the Prince of Wales' personal Beagle Basset CC1 XS770, Chipmunk T10 WP903 and an Andover, illustrates the unique breadth of skills required of The Queen's Flight's engineers.

During the first years of operation of a new aircraft, any problems encountered need particularly close investigation. The Senior Engineering Officer discusses a Gnome engine problem with a propulsion technician during the early period of service of the Wessex HCC Mk 4.

they occur: where a small engine or hydraulic oil-leak might be technically within limits, we will fix it to prevent the risk of an aborted task at a later date. Additional checks are also carried out on many of the aircraft systems prior to every Royal flight to give the best possible assurance that the aircraft will remain serviceable throughout its flying task.

Once the aircraft are technically perfect, they are cleaned inside and out and then inspected by the duty engineer to ensure that they are in immaculate condition for the next day's tasks. Two shifts of engineers work overnight and they see many dawns as they hand over to the day shift that will despatch the aircraft away again. Our record shows that these policies pay off, as our Andovers and Wessex experience less than half the rate of random equipment failures suffered by the same aircraft in normal squadron service.

The fixing of unserviceable aircraft, even when operating from base at RAF Benson, can often be a problem. The Royal flying task is very seasonal: there is almost no activity around Christmas and during August when the Royal Family take their holidays; by contrast, the spring and early summer months require all three Andovers and both Wessex to fly on most days. Our tasking assumes that the aircraft are one hundred per cent available, unless booked out many months in advance for scheduled maintenance.

There are many periods when perhaps two of the Andovers are away overseas on tour and our one remaining aircraft flies day after day for several weeks without a break. In these situations it is essential that replacement parts are immediately available and that the engineering support organisation can respond in a very quick time to deal with any problem that may arise.

The Queen's Flight does enjoy the advantages of a largely independent

Additional safety and survival equipment is carried on The Queen's Flight's aircraft, and is subject to the most careful checks. A floating radio-locator beacon is tested for correct operation.

engineering organisation controlled by a Squadron Leader engineer. This ensures the maximum integration and co-operation of the 120 men of the fifteen different trades under his command. The main aircraft engineering tradesmen are backed up by painters, ground equipment fitters, suppliers, motor transport fitters, drivers, carpenters and clerks, all of whom play an equally crucial role in achieving the task. Although the bulk of this team work a 'routine' day, they are difficult to keep away from the hangar when a problem arises. As an example, we recently had an Andover needing an engine and propeller change after the aircraft arrived at RAF Lyneham at eight o'clock one Saturday morning. The duty shift at base contacted off-duty personnel, and a replacement engine, propeller, tool-kit and engineering team were loaded in our truck and on the way before 11 am. Luckily, that day we had a spare Andover; any spare aircraft are always kept ready to go and this aircraft undertook the task. A second team worked overnight and into Sunday, when the repaired aircraft was air-tested and recovered from Lyneham to be ready for tasking again on Monday morning.

The esprit de corps of this excellent team constantly makes all the difference

between success and failure and is greatly enhanced by an awareness of the value of our role. All tradesmen have the opportunity to fly on several occasions in the year on tasks carrying members of the Royal Family. Every trade is also involved in the essential task of keeping the exterior of the aircraft looking immaculate. Each aircraft has a weekly full wash and polish, undertaken by personnel of Sergeant rank and below. This usually takes about an hour and the aircraft looks as if it is covered in a swarm of bees with about sixty tradesmen elbow-greasing to their utmost. Nevertheless, contrary to popular belief, the polishing of aircraft constitutes only a small part of our work, and the chance for all trades to work together to produce a gleaming machine is enjoyed by most.

Each man, from the aircraft cleaners to the most highly skilled aircraft fitters, is selected at interview from the best available in the RAF. All members of The Queen's Flight are volunteers and normally serve for a minimum of five years. Most of the engineers filling the important senior management posts have had their tours extended and have served between ten and fifteen years on The Queen's Flight; in this time they have risen from basic Junior Technician rank through Corporal, Sergeant to Chief Technician.

Components removed from the aircraft are tested and repaired in The Queen's Flight's own workshops. The flight systems tradesmen carry out intricate repairs to the Andover's delicate autopilot gyro equipment.

A few tradesmen of outstanding technical ability and personality are selected as aircraft Crew Chiefs. On both Andover and Wessex they fly with the aircraft at all times and are totally responsible for servicing the aircraft when away from base. On long overseas tours they are assisted by three other tradesmen and experience the tremendous challenge of maintaining our standards, often under the most rudimentary working conditions. Although the helicopter crewmen do not travel so extensively, they have an important additional role: because of the small size of the Wessex, they are also the stewards responsible for serving refreshments to the Royal passengers and for their comfort and safety on board. This unique combination can require them to be in immaculate order, serving coffee, perhaps only minutes after being in overalls while servicing the aircraft. This breadth of operational and engineering experience of the Crew Chiefs makes them excellent engineering managers. With the total dedication of all our personnel, this is a major factor in our ability to do the job.

In striving to maintain such levels of excellence, we are only keeping to the standards passed on to us by our predecessors on the Flight. Wing Commander Bill Lamb MVO, RAF (retd), served two tours as Engineering Officer, the first from 1950 to 1952. He remembers:

The seats, tables, carpets and interiors of the aircraft are always kept in immaculate condition. The crew seats are also used by Prince Philip and Prince Charles and receive the same detailed attention in the Interior Furnishings Section.

In 1950 The King's Flight was equipped with five Viking C2 aircraft, two of which were specially equipped and used exclusively for Royal flights (VL246 and VL247). Two aircraft were standard commercial 22-seat passenger aircraft and were used for support and training flights (VL232 and VL233). The fifth aircraft (VL248) was fitted out as a workshop, but by 1950 was 'mothballed' in storage. Externally, all the aircraft appeared alike and were maintained to the same high standard.

Parachutes were carried for all passengers and crew. Two eight-man dinghies were fitted in the upper rear of the engine nacelles. The fuel tanks were crash-proof and bullet-proof to the same pattern as the later Wellington bombers: the Viking wings and engine nacelles were in fact to the Wellington design of geodetic construction.

The flight-deck provided for an aircrew of four; a pilot and flight engineer at the dual controls and navigator and signaller at a sideways-facing desk. A crew lavatory and the galley with steward's position were aft of the flight-deck, as was the rearward-facing seat for the Captain of The King's Flight.

The Royal aircraft were kept in a state of basic readiness at all times as the engineering staff were given only short notice, usually less than twenty-four hours, of a Royal flight. When a Royal flight was notified, the aircraft was serviced to schedule requirements and then fully air-tested. The 'social engineering' was then carried out to ensure that the aircraft was immaculate both inside and out. The aircraft finish was bare unpainted aluminium and the whole exterior surface was hand-polished with metal polish and dusters. Not surprisingly, some skin panels had to be replaced over the years. All personnel took part in polishing, including clerks, typists and drivers, some sixty men in all; the whole task took about 200 man-hours. The undercarriage and radio aerials were chromium-plated and this saved a lot of cleaning work. There was never a problem of the chrome plating peeling off, as had been forecast by RAE.

The hangar was unheated and dimly lit by small ceiling-lights. Considered opinion agreed that winter in RAF hangars extended from 1 September to the following July. Certainly condensation was a major problem, especially when it came to polishing aeroplanes, and the only alternative to wet floors and walls was to keep the doors open and endure the blast. Aircraft servicing was carried out with the aid of torches and lead-lamps.

When preparation was completed, the aircraft was inspected by the Engineering Officer and the Flight Sergeant i/c Flight (only one Flight Lieutenant and one Flight Sergeant in 1950). This took about an hour and included checking documentation, fuel-state, appearance, correct flags, panels secure etc. There was no insurance factor applied in checking engineering work as the Captain's policy was 'one man, one job' and the full responsibility that went with it. This policy extended to one pilot being considered quite enough; second pilots were never carried, although the aircraft had dual controls.

The embarking or disembarking of the Royal Family was attended by personnel of The King's Flight as far as possible. Placing steps against an aircraft door may seem a simple enough task, but a combination of local airport workers and nervous officials was a recipe for embarrassment. The steps hitting the door-frame with a resounding thud, or being positioned a foot clear of the threshold, were experiences which led the Captain to direct that we do it ourselves. For aircraft positioned at London airport a 'steps party' was sent from Benson, while away from base, the flight engineer and the steward became

The flight-deck of one of the Vikings, VL247. Both the pilot and co-pilot had an excellent view from the cockpit.

A scene from 1951. Elbow-grease made the Vikings shine.

Even the Viking's propellers were polished to mirrors.

expert in quickly assembling dismantled steps carried in the hold. One near-miss occurred on an overseas tour when the local airport manager had special, hydraulically adjustable steps flown in from Cairo. The suspicious engineer required a full dress rehearsal and as the airport manager stepped from the aircraft, the steps gently subsided amidst a fountain of hydraulic fluid.

When an aircraft returned from a flight, it was re-prepared to a basic readiness state without delay, no matter what time of day or night it was. The fuel state was brought up to two-thirds full only, to prevent fuel having to be unloaded if the maximum disposable payload was required on the next flight. All galley equipment was re-prepared but stored in the hangar. Dust-sheets were placed on the furniture and floor and all doors locked.

During 1950 and 1951, probably due to the prolonged illness of The King, there were only ten or twelve Royal flights per month, which resulted in each

Right:
Polishing is a labour-intensive task but is very rewarding. A Viking's tail-cone receives the treatment.

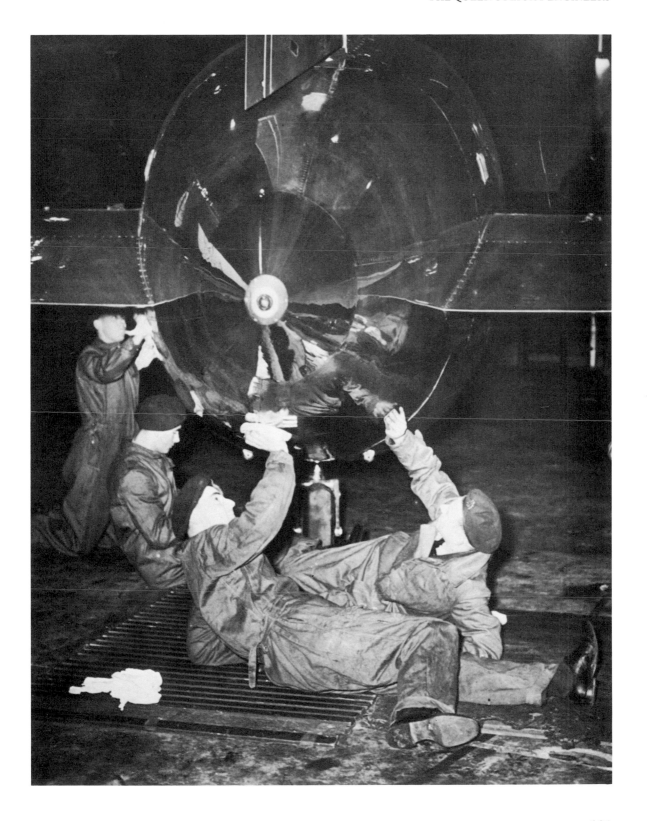

Royal aircraft flying about 200 hours per year. The other two aircraft flew about 400 hours per year on training and support flights. The life of main components between Major servicing or factory overhaul was: Viking airframe and associated components, 800 hours; Bristol Hercules 634 and components, 800 hours; DH propellers and components, 800 hours; wheels and tyres, 200 landings. It was realised that the level of aircraft utilisation would result in the two Royal aircraft taking four years between Major servicing while the two support aircraft would take only two years. The situation would soon arise where the support aircraft would have a better modification state than the Royal aircraft and would have newer components fitted.

A decision was made as a matter of internal policy that all 'lifed' components on the two Royal aircraft would be removed at half-life and fitted to the two support aircraft where the remaining life would be used prior to overhaul at the normal time. Higher authority was not consulted, and it was never the intention that components supplied to The King's Flight should only be used for half the normal life. However, this policy was subsequently adopted by the Air Ministry as one of the additional safety and reliability measures to be applied to The Queen's Flight aircraft.

Despite these measures, and however much care engineers take, they still need luck. Usually it is on their side. Recently, for example, one Andover returned from a three-week tour to the Far East on a Friday evening. It was during the busy summer months and the aircraft was needed to make two Royal flights on the following Monday and was tasked every day for the rest of the week as well. One of the several problems corrected overnight on Friday was an

The Queen's Flight – aircraft scheduled servicing. In addition to day-to-day flight servicing, The Queen's Flight's aircraft are serviced on the unit on a deeper scheduled basis. The Wessex is serviced according to its hours flown: Primary Star – every 150; Minor – every 300; Minor Star – every 600; Minor Two Star – every 1200; Major – every 2400 flying hours (about every 6 years). The Andover is serviced on a calendar basis with a flying hours backstop: Primary – 7½ months (up to 400); Minor – 15 months (up to 800); Minor Star – 30 months (up to 1600); Major – 60 months (up to 3200). The main servicings, re-paints and modification programmes are provisionally planned a year in advance, to the day, to fit in as far as possible with the expected flying hours and the main overseas tours.

The interior of the workshop/freighter Viking, VL248.

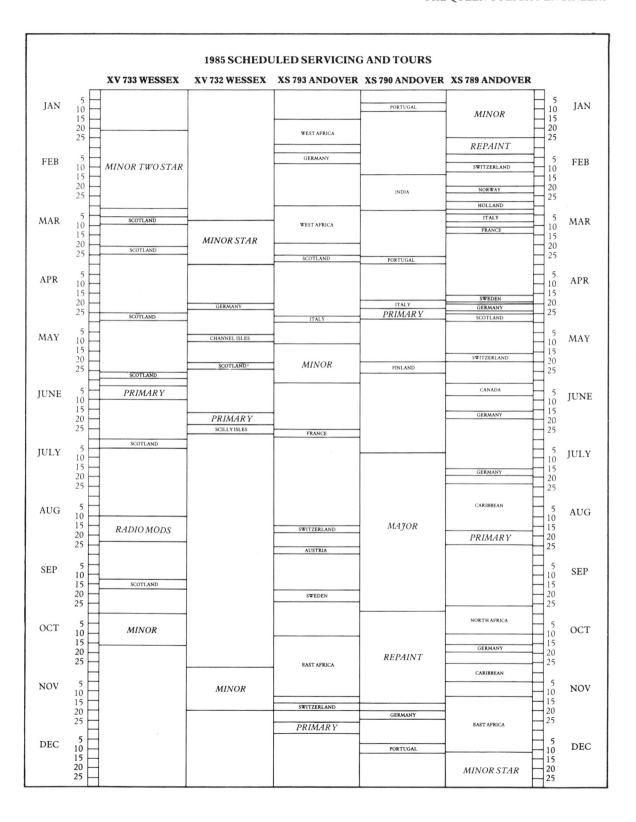

1985 SCHEDULED SERVICING AND TOURS

	XV 733 WESSEX	XV 732 WESSEX	XS 793 ANDOVER	XS 790 ANDOVER	XS 789 ANDOVER	
JAN				PORTUGAL	*MINOR*	JAN
	MINOR TWO STAR		WEST AFRICA		*REPAINT*	
FEB			GERMANY		SWITZERLAND	FEB
				INDIA	NORWAY	
					HOLLAND	
MAR	SCOTLAND		WEST AFRICA		ITALY	MAR
	SCOTLAND	*MINOR STAR*			FRANCE	
			SCOTLAND	PORTUGAL		
APR					SWEDEN	APR
	SCOTLAND	GERMANY		ITALY	GERMANY	
			ITALY	*PRIMARY*	SCOTLAND	
MAY		CHANNEL ISLES				MAY
	SCOTLAND	SCOTLAND'	*MINOR*	FINLAND	SWITZERLAND	
JUNE	*PRIMARY*				CANADA	JUNE
		PRIMARY			GERMANY	
		SCILLY ISLES	FRANCE			
JULY	SCOTLAND					JULY
					GERMANY	
AUG					CARIBBEAN	AUG
	RADIO MODS		SWITZERLAND	*MAJOR*	*PRIMARY*	
			AUSTRIA			
SEP						SEP
	SCOTLAND		SWEDEN			
OCT	*MINOR*				NORTH AFRICA	OCT
			EAST AFRICA	*REPAINT*	GERMANY	
NOV		*MINOR*			CARIBBEAN	NOV
			SWITZERLAND	GERMANY	EAST AFRICA	
			PRIMARY			
DEC				PORTUGAL		DEC
					MINOR STAR	

autopilot defect which required the aircraft to be air-tested first thing on Saturday. The duty engineer enquired of progress by phone during Saturday afternoon to be told, 'The engine change is going well.' An engine change normally takes two days and, knowing the busy week ahead, he thought the wags at work were having him on. No such thing. During the air test an engine had blown a compressor inter-stage seal and hot gas was leaking into the cowlings. The engine would have to go back to the manufacturers for repair. The engine change was accomplished without any trouble and the aircraft was soon ready for its busy week.

If the seal had blown a few flying hours earlier, we would have been stuck with an engine change down-route, probably somewhere in the Middle East. If it had not been for the autopilot problem, the aircraft would not have flown on Saturday and the engine fault would have occurred during a Royal task at the start of one of our busiest weeks of the year. This luck goes with the job. It helps us to meet the challenge which makes the task of the engineers on The Queen's Flight one of the most rewarding in the RAF.

7

HELICOPTER OPERATIONS

A helicopter task typically begins with the simple matter of a Royal Household contacting the Secretary to The Queen's Flight and booking a helicopter in advance. At least, it should be simple, but for maximum efficiency, attempts are made to dovetail flights throughout any one day if at all possible. Obviously, the workload is shared equally between the three crews who man the two Wessex HCC Mk 4s. However, HRH The Duke of Edinburgh and HRH The Prince of Wales have personal pilots allocated to them, who invariably fly with them. The Duke of Edinburgh always pilots the helicopter himself, and quite frequently so does the Prince of Wales.

Once a crew knows about a forthcoming flight, they make contact with one, some or all of the following: the Lord Lieutenant's office of the county involved, the county police and the organisers of the actual visit. It is actually the county police forces with whom we have our closest relationships. They are invariably involved with every visit, not only with the security aspects but, more importantly from our point of view, with the identification and organisation of all helicopter landing-sites that we use. Each force not only knows very well the criteria to which we work, but also treats us very well indeed when we visit its 'parish'.

Having gleaned as much relevant information as we can from our contacts, we arrange with them a mutually convenient date, hopefully well ahead of the actual visit, to carry out a proving flight. There is a popular misconception amongst the uninitiated that this is to check out our route and timings. This is not at all the case – in fact our main concern is to ensure that the proposed landing-site is acceptable from our point of view. Particular regard is given to the site's size, surface, approach and departure flight-paths and, if appropriate, its acceptability for night operations. The senior NCO in charge of our

invaluable support crews accompanies us on the proving flight – see the next chapter.

Whilst all interested parties are together, other details of the arrival and departure by helicopter are discussed, for example medical cover, security, crowd control and other arrival and departure details. We reassure organisers who are receiving a visit for the first time that we always endeavour to make our 'doors open' time to ensure that the Royal passenger steps out exactly on time to start the visit off on the right foot. We will *never* be early, we always say. We may perhaps be late, but, we emphasise, it won't be our fault. Don't panic, we tell them. No news is good news! Don't ring us, we'll ring you!

Not all venues need a proving flight – some which we regularly use can be accepted without further ado, provided that both ourselves and our police contacts are happy that nothing radical has changed since our last visit.

The selection and planning of a route for a helicopter flight may at first sight appear to be a simple operation of joining the departure and destination with a straight line. This would be the case when overflying terrain that is flat, unpopulated and weather-free, but as ideally all Royal helicopter flying requires maintaining visual contact with the ground, a number of factors influence the selection of the route.

As we fly at a relatively low altitude, the worst possible weather conditions are assumed at the planning stage and a route is selected avoiding high ground,

Since the allocation of two VVIP helicopters, Whirlwind HCC8s XN126 (illustrated) and XN127, to The Queen's Flight in November 1959, the use of helicopters by the Flight has consistently increased.

which in the case of mountainous areas can mean a twisting track, following valleys. The overflight of densely populated areas is also avoided, to reduce the nuisance factor.

A further consideration in route selection is that a protected zone (Royal Low-Level Corridor) is promulgated, warning other users of the airspace to keep clear or cease activities that would endanger or jeopardise the Royal helicopter. Airfields and danger areas are therefore avoided, to disrupt their activities as little as possible. In the case of large civilian airfields where it would be impractical to disrupt their activities, set controlled routes are flown. An example of this is the London area, where a large proportion of our flights are mounted.

Once the helicopter route has been selected, details will be published in the form of NOTAMs (Notice to Airmen), ideally ten days in advance of the flight, in order to provide a protected zone around the flight.

Various other agencies have to be informed of the movement, such as en route airfields for communications, operators of danger areas if closure is required, search and rescue organisations, and the Meteorological Office for en route weather forecasts.

The navigator for the flight, having decided on the route and after producing the necessary warning signals, will prepare mapping in the form of ¼ inch to 1 mile charts and a large-scale strip map of the entire route on which all hazards will be annotated, along with timing details to maintain a very strict schedule.

The loan from the Royal Navy of two Sikorsky Hoverfly Mk I Helicopters to The King's Flight in 1947, for carrying mail from Aberdeen airport to Balmoral, placed the Flight in the forefront of aviation progress.

The Queen Mother, seen here about to board a Whirlwind at Sandringham, has been a keen user of The Queen's Flight's helicopters since the first, the Dragonfly, was introduced. Note the flotation bags on the Whirlwind's undercarriage.

The Duke of Gloucester leaving Wessex HCC4 XV732 on a visit to an Army unit.

Lady Diana Spencer, accompanied by her fiancé, the Prince of Wales, making her first journey with The Queen's Flight in one of the Wessex HCC4s, to Cheltenham on 27 March 1981.

The Duke of Edinburgh at the controls of one of The Queen's Flight's Wessex during a visit to Hawker Siddeley Dynamics at Hatfield. A qualified helicopter pilot, Prince Philip normally flies the Wessex when on engagements.

Other specialist maps are also prepared, depending on the area to be overflown.

At the planning stage, the possibility of bad weather during the flight, which would make it impossible to maintain visual contact with the ground, is considered. A plan is produced to carry out the flight under Instrument Flying Rules (in cloud) with details of instrument let-downs to airfields close to the destinations – the idea being either that the Royal passenger should disembark at that airfield and complete the journey by road, or that after the let-down, we continue but beneath the cloud.

The weather on the day of the Royal Flight is always in the lap of the gods, probably the only factor over which we have absolutely no control.

Royal helicopter flights rarely start and finish at airfields. On the contrary, our pick-up points are usually in Central London or at one of the Royal residences scattered across the country, and our destination could be anywhere, literally *anywhere*! This means that we must be able to rely on visual contact with the ground for the last stages of the journey, so fog, very low cloud or icing conditions are factors which will give us significant problems and probably force us into cancelling a Royal flight. If this is the case, a 'no go' decision is made as early as possible in order for the Royal Household to make alternative arrangements. Even if weather curtails the early part of a day's programme, we do monitor the conditions and try to pick up the schedule.

Notwithstanding any weather problems, the actual flight is by now very much a known quantity in that virtually all contingencies have been covered by all the intricate planning preceding it. Note that I say 'virtually all', for it would be a

foolish man to be complacent, particularly where aviation is concerned. Never let it be said that we don't start every day with our eyes open.

The majority of our helicopter operations are in essence quite straightforward, but occasionally a more complex operation will come our way which requires significant liaison with other agencies outside our normal sphere.

Visits by the members of the Royal Family to Northern Ireland invariably make use of our helicopters. These visits normally involve flights to several different venues, all in the same day, so the speed between sites and the security en route afforded by a helicopter are invaluable advantages to all concerned. Usually our VVIP arrives at Belfast by Queen's Flight Andover and is then taken on tour by the awaiting helicopter, accompanied by other units of the security forces. All the arrangements are made on a very strict 'need to know' basis, so our visits to the Province come as a great surprise to most people.

A recent tour of the Western Isles by the Prince and Princess of Wales proved to be a major logistics exercise. Because of the nature of the terrain and

On 11 July 1982, the Prince of Wales, a qualified helicopter pilot, flew a Queen's Flight Wessex on to the temporary troopship SS Canberra in Southampton Water on her return to the UK from service during the Falklands Campaign.

The Queen made her first helicopter flight, in Wessex XV732, from HMS *Fife, the escort to* HMY *Britannia, to Hillsborough Castle, returning the following day in XV733 (pictured).*

difficulty of access to many of the sites involved, the support of a Sea King helicopter from the Search and Rescue Flight at RAF Lossiemouth was enlisted for the three-day tour. Their involvement enabled us to pre-position our support crews ahead of the Royal helicopter by a series of leap-frog manoeuvres. Additionally, the Sea King carried a medic throughout and acted as search and rescue back-up during our flights over water and mountainous terrain. Indeed, without their participation, the intense three-day schedule would have been impossible and the number of venues would certainly have had to be reduced.

HM The Queen does not normally fly in the helicopters. However, during her visits to Northern Ireland in August 1977 and to Normandy in June 1984, we had the honour of carrying Her Majesty to her venues, thereby easing the security problem considerably and making what in both cases would have been a major logistical exercise into a relatively simple matter.

Embarrassing moments are not really in the terms of reference of The Queen's Flight – at least, none which would be readily admitted. However, incidents do occur which could fall into this category. One such occasion was precipitated by the unpredictability of our arch-enemy, the weather.

We were flying Their Royal Highnesses The Prince and Princess of Wales from West Yorkshire to Central London. Because of the distance involved, combined with the number of passengers carried, a planned en route refuel was organised at East Midlands airport. The forecast was not wonderful, but nevertheless suitable for an instrument approach into East Midlands if the weather proved unsuitable for a visual transit.

The Princess of Wales has made frequent use of The Queen's Flight helicopters, an ideal means of transport for fulfilling a crowded engagement calendar with speed and convenience. Here, Her Royal Highness is seen carrying out her first visit to Northern Ireland.

To cut a long story short, the instrument approach option was taken in view of updated actual reports from East Midlands whilst en route, which indicated that the weather situation was deteriorating somewhat faster than had been predicted. The weather at RAF Finningley, however, remained good as a diversion – unfortunately, it would be back the way we had come.

During the instrument approach to East Midlands, the weather 'socked in' in no uncertain terms, much to everyone's surprise. A diversion to the known good weather at RAF Finningley was commenced without any further ado. It must be said that in a situation like this the crew feel a great deal of sympathy for the hierarchy of the diversion airfield, imagining the pandemonium at having to organise a Royal visit with only fifteen minutes warning – still, if you can't take a joke, etc!

After landing, the Royal party were whisked away to join a scheduled train passing through the local station on its way to London. The helicopter was refuelled to maximum capacity now that it was without passengers, and took off with enough fuel to fly through the bad weather to its base at RAF Benson. After leaving RAF Finningley, the helicopter was able to fly visually for several miles before having to climb and continue back to base.

A few days later, when the same crew flew the Prince and Princess again, they were very red-faced when the lady herself enquired how it was that she saw a bright red Wessex helicopter whizzing past the hastily commandeered 'Royal train carriage' at a great rate of knots, heading the same way as they were? – It turned out that 'Sod's Law' applies to The Queen's Flight as well as to everyone else – how were we to know it was their train? Our blushes were proved unnecessary when we saw the tongue in cheek and wry smile!

8

THE HELICOPTER
SUPPORT SECTION

Quite early in its helicopter operations, the benefit of The Queen's Flight having its own crash-rescue and firefighting facilities became obvious. There was a real need to have the basic capability at the sites which were being used throughout the country, and the extra benefit of using dedicated men who knew the Flight's operation and who could take on the responsibility of organising the landing-sites before the arrival of the helicopter was soon appreciated. They are now vital to the safe, timely and polished arrivals we make with the helicopters.

The Fire Section was formed in 1954 with two Land-Rovers carrying dry-powder extinguisher packs, each crewed by a Corporal and a Senior Aircraftman, both firemen. In 1960 a third Land-Rover and crew were added.

With the change to the Wessex Mk 4s in 1969, we took delivery of three specialist vehicles. The manning was now one Sergeant, two Corporals and six airmen. One Land-Rover was retained. The Fire Section soon became the Helicopter Support Section, a title which more accurately described their function, but the main reason for their existence remained firefighting and crash-rescue, so the vehicles were, and their present versions are now, crewed entirely by RAF firemen. The crew of a helicopter support vehicle (HSV to us) is a Corporal and two airmen.

Those original HSVs served us well for sixteen years. They were built on a Bedford chassis, with four-wheel drive for cross-country capability, and were petrol-engined. They carried a hundred gallons of light water (foam), which an engine-driven fire pump could deliver through two branch lines, and as much of the equipment of the professional fireman such as axes, hydraulic cutting equipment, ladder, stretcher, first-aid kit, as reasonably could be fitted into this type of vehicle. For their support operation on the landing-site, they carried a large canvas 'H' marker, lengths of rubberised matting which could be pinned

securely to bridge the gap over wet ground between helicopter steps and car or hard-standing, a lighting system for night helicopter operations, radio to communicate directly with the helicopters, and up to 198 gallons of aviation fuel, in jerrycans, which could be hand-poured through the appropriate filter into the helicopter tanks. (So that's why firemen need to be fit!) These HSVs had a large cabin in which it was envisaged that heavy spares (even a complete engine-change unit for a helicopter) could be carried – they never were, but the cabin gave enough space for modified aircraft seats to be fitted to give cruise comfort for the crew. The HSVs also had a 24-volt system which could provide engine starting power for the helicopter from a large-capacity battery installation.

We still needed a smaller vehicle to solve the problem of access to sites via narrow lanes and gateways, over bridges with load-bearing limitations, or on small ferries. The Land-Rover was changed for a standard Airfield Crash Rescue Truck (TACR Mk 2, a six-wheeled stretched Range Rover with a 200-gallon foam tank) in 1977, and then in 1979, to cope with our steadily increasing task, a second TACR2 and an extra crew were established.

The vintage HSVs were replaced in 1985. The new ones have all of the same facilities, but better – twice the foam capacity, a diesel engine, a pumped aircraft-refuelling system, a site light on a rising stem with a tremendous light output for illumination of the scene, and even a domestic water boiling unit to replenish the helicopter's vacuum flasks.

It is of great benefit to The Queen's Flight to have its own helicopter support crews pre-positioned at landing sites. Their experience of operations is not only of valuable assistance to the police and visit organisers, but it is a great advantage to the aircrew to be in radio contact with the Flight's 'men on the spot', who have set up the site, providing the mandatory crash rescue vehicle (illustrated) and fuel 'on tap' if required.

A Westland Wessex HCC4 demonstrates the ability of the helicopter to reach parts that other means of transport could not. The Wessex HCC4, larger and more powerful than the Whirlwind, greatly enhanced the rotary-winged capability of The Queen's Flight.

So what we have now is a Sergeant in charge of five vehicles and four crews. This is how it works.

As you will have gathered by now, the usage rate of the helicopters can peak, with both of them flying on tasks for many consecutive days. Let's look at a typical task for one helicopter on one day which might be to carry a passenger from a country residence to an engagement in, say, the Midlands in the morning, then on to a second engagement, perhaps in East Anglia, then return to central London in the evening, which we will assume to be after dark.

This clearly means the use of four landing sites. We will be familiar with the starting-point and with the central London site, but the two other venues could require considerable research and a reconnaissance visit to find suitable sites.

The Sergeant in charge of the section will always have accompanied the proving flight, to discuss possible approaches and the optimum landing-point with the pilot, to check the means of access for the HSV, to make a sketch of the site, to find somewhere for the firemen to change from uniforms into firesuits, to note telephone contact numbers and generally to arm himself with all he needs to brief the crew of the HSV which he will allocate.

Closer to the date, the Sergeant organises vehicles and crews for the week in which the task falls. For this task three vehicles will suffice — one to cover the departure point in the morning, then proceed to the London site to set up the area for a night approach, the other two for the other two sites. (You can imagine that the planning becomes much more complicated when we consider

the movements of the other helicopter on the same day, then co-ordinate this day with the preceding and subsequent ones.) The Corporals of the crews are briefed by the Sergeant, and whenever possible by the aircrew. They pick their own routes and decide on their departure time, planning always to arrive on site at least one hour before the scheduled landing time for the helicopter.

So, involved in the task are three HSVs – call them A, B and C – and four sites, 1, 2, 3 and 4. Crew A drives to Site 1. They get there before the helicopter leaves base, having driven through areas of fog, but finding that Site 1 is clear, the Corporal telephones this information back to base where it is gratefully received by the pilot as confirmation of the met man's best guess.

Crew B meanwhile arrives at Site 2 (the helicopter is still en route to Site 1), where they are provided with a room in which to change, and even a welcome

Sultan Qaboos of Oman, one of many overseas VIPs carried by The Queen's Flight's helicopters, alighting to find the visit organisation running smoothly, in no small way due to the support crew. The site has been assessed and the 'H' marker laid by the support crew – although the Wessex has an inaccurate wheel actually on the marker!

cup of tea, before proceeding to the adjoining sports field which happens to be an ideal landing-site. The ground is firm and dry – no need for any matting, just peg out an 'H' so that everybody knows where the helicopter will touch down (including the pilot).

While they are doing this, the local police Inspector tells the Corporal that a hundred or so youngsters will be turning up soon from the nearby school, and where does he suggest they stand? There are a few dozen people gathering along one side, and he'll have to ask them to move as the helicopter will be approaching right over that area; the ambulance has arrived and parked beside the HSV; the Managing Director wants to know where to put the cars; the Corporal is trying to explain that despite where the helicopter door was on the proving flight, the wind is now blowing from the opposite direction so the door will be on *this* side, but in any case there will be plenty of time to move forward. And 'Would you like to stay well back over there, sir, until the rotor stops?' He's seen it all before – wet grass-cuttings, dust, hats and skirts all on the move, displaced by six tonnes of helicopter down-draught. At least there are no arguments about red carpets today. This one is easy; he still remembers being swamped by 3000 people in a public park the first time we carried a certain young princess.

With the spectators safely organised in a good viewing position and the HSV strategically parked, the crew await the radio call from the helicopter, fending off the inevitable question of 'Will it/he/she/they be on time?' with the usual 'Yes, unless we hear otherwise' or 'No news is good news'.

The Lord Lieutenant for the county has arrived to meet and greet HRH, then, with about fifteen miles to run, the helicopter duly calls: 'Rover Zero Four, this is Kittyhawk Five. We'll be on time.' The HSV driver acknowledges, passes the suggested landing direction to the pilot, adds any relevant reminders such as 'low wires on the approach', and alerts the Corporal who will be on field to marshal the helicopter down and direct/invite the meeters and greeters towards the helicopter as it shuts down. Just as the rotor stops, the door is opened (on time to the second, of course) from within by the Crew Chief, who lowers the steps for HRH to descend. One more Royal flight completed.

When HRH has departed the scene and the immediate interest in the aircraft has died down, the firemen provide chocks for the aircraft and help the Crew Chief fit intake and exhaust covers. A top-up of fuel is needed at this stage of the day, so the HSV is carefully positioned, electrically earthed and bonded to the helicopter, the fuel-hose is run out and, when the Crew Chief has checked a fuel sample to ensure no water content, the firemen dispense the required amount – all carefully metered and logged, of course.

Meanwhile, Crew C is on the way to Site 3, having left base in the late morning. They are squeezed into the somewhat cramped interior of a Range Rover, a much smaller vehicle than the Bedford HSV, but still a heavy machine with its 200-gallon water tank and a load of equipment, including spare aircraft batteries. Even so, it is capable of moving along quite briskly under the power

of a big V8 petrol engine, but you are very aware of the body-roll when cornering with a ton of water aboard. Access to their site is via a low archway which a Bedford could not negotiate; the landing-site is a fairly small area quite close to the building which HRH is visiting, but with clear approaches for the helicopter over open countryside apart from the odd tree. The helicopter will land beside the path here and HRH can walk straight into the building.

It will be nearly dusk when the helicopter departs from here towards London. Crew C will then drive further north to make a pre-arranged night stop, putting them within reach of their next task near Sheffield tomorrow.

In London, Crew A arrived in mid-afternoon after their 120-mile drive, parked the HSV in the usual secure area, had plenty of time for a meal and were at Site 4 in daylight, setting up the familiar night landing-aid. This is a geometric pattern of battery-operated lights which delineate an approach-path direction and safe angle clear of obstructions which the helicopter will be able to recognise and follow, even on a dirty wet night with a failed landing-lamp. In the absence of any other message, the Corporal will switch on the lights thirty

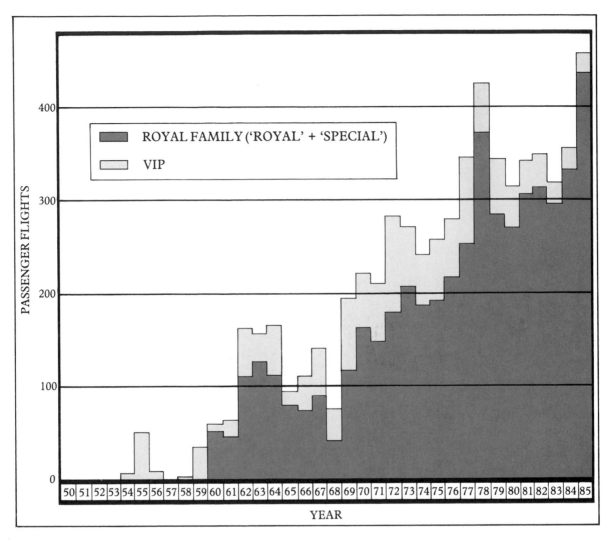

minutes before the helicopter is due – he knows it could be early on the return flight as timing is not important on the home run. The HSV is also equipped with an eye-catching strobe light which can be used to assist the helicopter crew with their initial identification of the site.

The expected call eventually comes: 'Rover Zero Five, Kittyhawk Five with you in five minutes.'

'Roger, Kittyhawk Five. Approach one nine zero degrees. Glidepath at ten degrees.'

The helicopter lands – usual shutdown routine – a chauffeur drives the car almost to the cabin door – HRH descends from the cabin as the last few thousand engine rpm whine down – smiles thanks towards the cockpit and exchanges gentle banter about the time-keeping or the weather – boards car to the Palace before evening engagement (how do they keep up the pace?).

Use of The Queen's Flight's helicopters for Royal and Special flights has heavily increased since the early 1970s, underlining their importance and practicality for fulfilling The Queen's Flight's 'short-haul' commitments. In the same period, VIP use by members of the Government and others has tended to remain fairly static, decreasing in the 1980s as commercial companies and No. 32 Squadron shouldered some of this burden.

By now, the fog is beginning to threaten again, so some more fuel is taken on to increase the diversion options for the helicopter, plugging in the HSV's battery power now for the helicopter's lights and for the re-start. All this takes no more than fifteen minutes, and the helicopter is away for the last hop back to base. One of the firemen from Crew A is given a lift back in the helicopter, leaving the Corporal and one man to return with the HSV – not much more than an hour's run in reasonable traffic this evening.

Of course, they're all out again tomorrow. The aircraft will be serviced overnight; and the vehicles will be immaculate in their dark blue finish when they depart again. The wives are remarkably understanding, and with luck, half of the firemen will get both Saturday and Sunday off this weekend. Two crews will have to depart on Sunday to be in Scotland on Tuesday – but it could all change before then.

That was a simple day. We used nine sites one day last month (and only one of them twice), and seven the next day. It all went like clockwork, as it usually does, but you can guess what a flurry of activity is generated when one vehicle suffers even a minor breakdown. Then the initiative is with the Corporal whose vehicle it is, but we get the same sort of response from our MT section as the engineers give to an aircraft with a snag, and if it can possibly be fixed in time, it is.

As well as all points between Land's End and John o'Groats, we've taken Royal passengers in our helicopters (and therefore needed firemen on site with their equipment) to the top of Snowdon, to the Western Isles (even St Kilda, which is off the top left-hand corner of most people's maps of the UK), to the Shetlands, the Orkneys, the Channel Isles and the Scillies. We sometimes need a little help from other friendly services to get them there with their kit, but there they are, with portable fire-extinguishers and a radio (hand-held now): 'Kittyhawk Seven from Rover One . . .'

9

STEWARDING AND INTERIORS

One of the smallest yet most important elements of The Queen's Flight is the Flight Stewards' section, an enthusiastic and dedicated team of four Flight Stewards who look to the comfort and needs of the Royal Family when travelling in the Andovers and Wessex of The Queen's Flight. Specially selected for Royal duties on the basis of the highest professional standards and personal qualities, the Stewards will have previously served for at least one tour of VIP duty with either No. 10 or No. 32 Squadrons of the Royal Air Force, before joining The Queen's Flight for a minimum tour of five years. In professional terms their work is extremely demanding and embraces many more facets than that of their civilian counterparts or other Flight Stewards within the Service. Collectively and individually, the Flight Stewards must be able to perceive and anticipate the in-flight needs of the Royal Family, their Households and the flight crew; it is hoped that the other aspect of their duties, the safety of passengers during an in-flight emergency, will never have to be put into practice, but regular training ensures that the Flight Stewards are able to respond appropriately in the very unlikely event of such a need arising.

Much of the Flight Stewards' daily routine involves planning and preparing for Royal flights, and even a short-duration flight within the United Kingdom will require considerable preparation and careful attention to detail. For a short journey or series of journeys, the knowledge gained by experience of the Royal Family's likes and dislikes allows the Stewards to cater appropriately, without constant reference to the Royal Households. The catering requirements are then ordered from a civilian 'in-flight' caterer and collected in purpose-built 'air-larder' boxes early in the morning of the flight, the food subsequently being served as required from the Andover's small galley.

For Royal Tours overseas, the Flight Stewards need to maintain a much

```
.BEXQFRR 121200 ND DEC 85
ATTEN EXECUTIVE CHEF FM THE QUEENS FLIGHT
FLIGHT NO.8521   DATE 28 DEC 85   A/C NO. XS790
CAPTAIN SQN LDR WILLIAMS   STEWARD MALM STOKES
CATERING REQD LUNCH FOR ROYAL PARTY AS FOLLOW
TWELVE LUNCH TRAYS COMPLETE TO GOLD STANDARDS WITH MAIN COURSE
IN BULK AND EIGHT INCH PLATES PROVIDED EMPTY
STARTERS...SIX GUINEA FOWL TERRINE...SIX SMOKED SALMON
DESSERTS...ELEVEN KIRCH GATEAUX...ONE FRESH FRUIT
MAIN COURSE...SIX PORTIONS SCAMPI ALICE IN FOIL
...SIX PORTIONS VEAL IN FOIL
ONE LARGE FOIL RICE
ONE LARGE FOIL BROCCOLI
ONE LARGE FOIL SPINACH
ONE PORTION CREAM ON EACH TRAY
ONE LARGE CHEESE TRAY BISCUITS AND CELERY
ONE LARGE FRUIT TRAY
ONE FOIL FRESHLY PREPARED MELBA TOAST
TWELVE ASSORTED BREAD ROLLS
FORTY EIGHT BUTTER PATS
TWO LITRES FRESH ORANGE JUICE
CATERING REQD FOR DAY TWO
TWENTY FOUR CUTLERY PACKS
TEN MARMALADE PORTIONS
SIX PINTS FRESH MILK
FOUR LEMONS
DRY ICE
RAF TRANSPORT WILL COLLECT AT 0700 LOCAL
PLEASE ACK BEXQFRR SOONEST
```

A routine telex order from The Queen's Flight to the catering contractor for a Royal flight.

closer liaison with the Household staffs, to determine the in-flight catering requirements for a series of trips which could cover a four-week period and which must be planned around the formal lunches and dinners which will be attended by the Royal party in the host countries visited. The Flight Steward's planning will start as soon as the provisional flight itinerary is produced, some two to three months in advance of the journey, and will take into account the time of day and duration of each flight, availability of fresh food and potable water, variety in the menus and any special requests from the Royal party.

Determining the requirements is the simplest part of the exercise; the difficulties arise in actually obtaining the necessary supplies once outside the United Kingdom and, perhaps, away from the established air-routes. Provisioning can come from the dedicated 'in-flight' caterers at major airfields or, where facilities are known to be wanting, food and beverages may have to be flown in by scheduled airline from our caterer in London; this requires careful study of airline timetables to ensure that the provisions arrive before our departure, whilst still remaining suitably fresh.

The interior of DH89 Rapide G-ADDD, fitted out for the Prince of Wales. There was hardly much scope for in-flight catering. The cabin clock and altimeter in the centre now hang in the office of the Captain of The Queen's Flight.

The Vickers Viastra X G-ACCC was the first aircraft to be ordered in a special version for a member of the Royal Family. Great attention was paid to comfort, as evinced by Vickers' own report on the interior furnishings: 'To meet the special requirement of utilising the space in the cabin to the greatest advantage and of making it as comfortable as possible for long journeys, the whole of the equipment, with the exception of cigarette lighters, has been designed and manufactured in the works. The furnishing of the cabin has been artistically carried out in veneered woods, all Empire grown. Between the panelling and the Balsa wood bearers a layer of chamois leather has been placed to lower the resonating sounds. The whole surface of the inner side of the outer cabin skin is covered with special Hairlok and dry zero blankets of varying thickness, specially produced by the builders. This coupled with a special fireproofed airtight paper partition and double thickness insulated windows has produced a cabin quieter than an express train. Special care has been taken to see that the Air Ministry regulations as regards fireproofing have been adhered to and so allow smoking.'

The elegant interior of one of the DH95s brought new standards to Royal flying.

Seats in a Royal saloon of one of The King's Flight's Vikings. The Royal cabins in The King's and The Queen's Vikings each had eight seats in facing pairs, in two saloons.

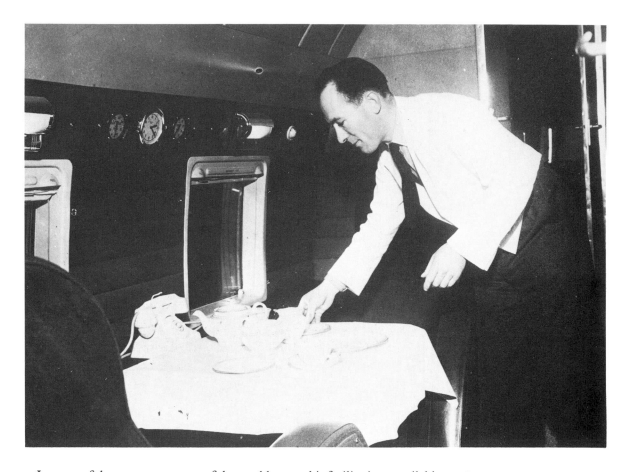

In some of the remoter corners of the world, even this facility is unavailable and the Stewards can encounter primitive catering establishments which are unhygienic and do not measure up to the standards required for Royal catering. In this situation, ingredients are purchased in local shops and markets, and food is prepared from the basic raw materials to produce meals of the highest standards of hygiene and nutritional value. The importance of all this careful planning cannot be over-emphasised and whatever catering service is eventually decided upon, it is this attention to detail which will ensure the very best of service wherever in the world the flight may be.

About one week before departure, the final and precise catering plan will have evolved and the detailed requirements will be telexed to the appropriate agencies along the route. Once the flight is under way, the preparation of meals, given the limited storage and cooking facilities of the Andover galley, is a difficult task. The area is very restricted in size and is equipped with only one small grill and a hot plate, a hot cup unit and a boiler, all of which will only work when airborne. To produce a five-course meal to the very high standards required needs more than just the ingredients and ingenuity; flair and imagination are essential qualities expected of a Steward on The Queen's Flight.

Sergeant Griffiths, a steward of The King's Flight, laying a table for tea in one of the Royal Vikings.

126

Thirty or so years on, another Sergeant Griffiths, a Queen's Flight steward, photographed with tea prepared aboard one of the Royal Andovers.

Thirty or so years on, another Sergeant Griffiths, a Queen's Flight steward, photographed with tea prepared aboard one of the Royal Andovers.

Nevertheless, the spartan galley of the Andover is a great improvement over that of the earlier Vikings, as remembered by a former member of the Flight, who provides an insight into cabin services in the 1950s:

While the aircraft exterior was being polished, the three stewards prepared the interior and loaded the cutlery, glass and crockery into special racks. Catering supplies were prepared by the same stewards in the galley in the hangar. The stewards were in fact batmen/waiters who were paid 1/6 per day (7½p) flying pay. Food was a problem, as rationing was strictly observed by the Royal Family; in 1950 bread was rationed and the meat ration was 10d (4p) worth per week. Eggs were sometimes obtainable and the King enjoyed a four-minute egg. In an unpressurised aircraft the temperature of boiling water varies with altitude, but such was the engineering expertise available that the galley displayed a graph showing the boiling time of a 'four-minute egg' at various altitudes. Incidentally, the egg was boiled in the hot-water geyser, but it was washed first so the tea was not polluted.

The Andover galley is situated immediately behind the flight-deck and thereafter the aircraft interior is sub-divided into three compartments: A, B, C.

Compartment A is forward and next to the galley. It includes a large pannier which has been specially adapted and designed by the Interior Furnishing Section of The Queen's Flight to enlarge and enhance the preparation surfaces available to the Steward; also included are a table and four seats, mainly for the use of supplementary crew such as security and engineering support staff. A curtained bulkhead separates compartment A from B. In this latter section are two tables, each with four seats and two small wardrobes, one each to port and starboard side of the centre aisle. Compartment B is used mainly by members of the Royal Household such as private secretaries, personal detective and the flight Commodore. It is segregated by a partition and door from compartment C. This section is for the exclusive use of Royal passengers and comprises two tables, each with two chairs. To the rear of the compartment is an entrance vestibule where the Flight Steward positions himself to greet the Royal passengers as they board the aircraft.

The memories of a previous member of the Flight provide another interesting insight into the Viking aircraft of the 1950s:

Accommodation in the Royal aircraft provided for eight passengers in two saloons, each equipped with four large armchair seats; two facing forward, two facing aft. The seats were remarkable in that they were steel-framed and stressed to 25g with a parachute cunningly concealed in the upholstery. The seats were also remarkably uncomfortable, a matter on which HRH The Duke of Gloucester expressed forthright views. Between each pair of seats was a white GPO telephone which connected to a small telephone exchange located at the seat provided for the Captain of The King's Flight, Sir Edward Fielden. The telephones provided only internal communication. To the rear of the saloons was a lavatory and wardrobe and at the extreme rear of the aircraft a small cabin with a divan bed.

The décor was royal blue for carpets, curtains and upholstery, with walls, ceilings and doors in cream PVC, the whole effect being one of spacious luxury, rather after the style of the Royal Daimler cars.

Whilst it is fascinating to reflect on the past, the Flight Stewards now look forward to working in the BAe 146, which, as might be expected, is better equipped and far more spacious than the Andover, allowing this élite team to continue to cater for the comfort and safety of all passengers effectively, discreetly and to the very highest standards.

10

'IT WAS KIND OF QUIET OUTSIDE . . .'

The unique qualities of The Queen's Flight inspire a special esprit de corps among its ex-members. To foster this, The Queen's Flight Association was formed in 1982. One of its members, Wing Commander W.T. Bussey LVO, OBE, BEM, RAF (retd), served no less than three tours with the Flight – the first as a Leading Aircraftman from 1939 to 1941, the third as a Squadron Leader and the Senior Engineering Officer from 1955 to 1961. As a flight mechanic, he was closely involved with Royal flying in the early days of the war:

The Hudson aircraft, N7263 underwent several modifications on receipt in August 1939 to suit it for its role. Most of the modifications were done at Farnborough. Radio sets were duplicated in an effort to ensure absolute communication. An IFF set was fitted and three Vickers K guns were added to its armament, one in the nose-cone and one on either side of the rear fuselage at window positions. Had the threatened invasion of the country materialised, bomb-racks were available, and it was anticipated that the aircraft could have been used for this purpose if needed. Fuselage fuel-tanks were manufactured and fitted by the Cunliffe-Owen aircraft company at Southampton to give the aeroplane a long-range capacity. All the extra equipment was stored at Benson.

After the fall of France the normal complement of the aircraft was: pilot, Wing Commander Fielden; Jenkins, engineer, in the right-hand cockpit seat; Figg, wireless operator; Reed, dorsal turret gunner; Bussey, front gunner; Morley, acting steward and side-gunner. Jenkins would move to the other side-gunner position in the event of enemy aircraft in the vicinity.

Our passengers were mainly HRH The Duke of Kent, who was on the staff of Inspector General of the Royal Air Force at that time, and TRH The Duke and Duchess of Gloucester. On one occasion we carried the King of Norway and another passenger, I believe, was a Belgian princess. (Because of the close security condition that prevailed we were never told in advance who our passengers would be.)

On 9 August 1941, we had HM King George VI on board from Inverness to Hatston in the Orkney Isles. On this occasion we were escorted by a Hurricane squadron of Czech pilots who, being so proud of being given the honour of escorting the King, orbited the aircraft rather too closely in vics of three, to the consternation of the Captain. During the flight, German aircraft had attacked shipping along the Orkney coast and this had alerted the Royal Navy in Scapa Flow. Having dropped our passenger, our flight-path took us near to Scapa as we departed the island, and a trigger-happy Naval gunner took a shot at us, much to the Captain's annoyance.

On another journey from Scotland, we had passed Barrow-in-Furness in bad weather and low cloud on our way to Rhyl. As we dropped out of cloud to search for our pinpoint, we found ourselves right over a convoy heading for Liverpool. Again we had a very hostile reception, but we were lucky. As the Captain commented, 'Thank God the Navy cannot shoot!'

We experienced two enemy air-raids on Benson airfield during the Battle of Britain. On one of these a stick of bombs straddled the airfield, the last one exploding near the hangar and spraying it with debris. One dropped within feet of the hangar but did not explode. Several air-raid warnings were given and during these the Captain always sat at the entrance to the shelter with a Thompson machine-gun at the ready.

During the invasion threat we made adaptors to enable the three Vickers K guns normally carried on the aircraft to be used for defence of the hangar.

Earlier, during the Phoney War, Jenkins and I were returning to the aircraft

Lockheed Hudson Mk I N7263, seen at Hatson in the Orkneys on 9 May 1941 with HRH The Duke of Kent, who had become a staff officer in RAF Training Command a year earlier. N7263 was finished in the standard RAF early-war scheme of Dark Earth/Dark Green/Sky Type S, with roundels in six positions, but bore no unit codes.

Percival Q6 P5634 was allocated to The King's Flight on 15 March 1940 for light liaison duties. It was subsequently used by the C-in-C RAF Bomber Command and was re-allocated to RAF Halton on 25 May 1942 after The King's Flight disbanded.

at Paris airport in heavy rain. The French guard was standing under the mainplane out of the weather. As we alighted from the vehicle he attempted to shoulder his arms and, in doing so, managed to push his bayonet through the mainplane. After this incident, on Royal tours overseas we always insisted that bayonets were not carried by local troops guarding our aircraft.

A similar incident was to occur at Jesselton, North Borneo, on 1-2 March 1959 during Prince Philip's world tour. After convincing, with great difficulty, the local guard commander that bayonets must not be fitted whilst his troops were in the aircraft vicinity, Squadron Leader K. Hannah and I returned at dusk to check, to find the guard without bayonets but peacefully cooking their evening meal on an open fire almost under our aircraft wing-tip. Having put that right, we were awakened at two o'clock next morning with the news that one of the guards had accidentally loosed off a round from his rifle which had penetrated the leading edge of the mainplane and scored the top of the cockpit as it passed. We effected the necessary repair and Prince Philip was able to carry on his tour early next morning as scheduled.

Royal flying during the 1939-45 War was still supervised by the Captain of The King's Flight, Edward Fielden, who retained this appointment even though the Flight itself was disbanded.

Air Commodore J.L. Mitchell LVO, DFC, AFC, AE, RAF (retd) − not to be

131

confused with his namesake of the same rank who later became Captain of The Queen's Flight – was involved in wartime Royal flying, including King George VI's dramatic and hazardous visit to North Africa in June 1943:

I was posted to No. 12 OTU at Benson in early May 1940 for operational training on Fairey Battles, at this time supporting No. 98 Squadron at Rheims. I was then an Acting Pilot Officer Observer, one of the first to be commissioned into the RAFVR. On reporting to my flight I was despatched, inevitably as bog-rat, to fetch the Oxometer. My journey round the station to find this mythical piece of equipment took me past a hangar in which half the floor-space was screened off from the Battles. I found it contained a Lockheed Hudson (N7263) and a Percival Q6 (P5634). These aircraft were the residue of The King's Flight, conveniently located near London, Windsor and the home of the Air Equerry and Captain of the Flight. This Hudson was fitted with its Atlantic ferry tanks, and turretted. Coincidentally, as it turned out for me, the crew of this aircraft was found from No. 24 Squadron at Hendon, the VIP transport squadron of the RAF.

In May 1943, three years later, I was posted to No. 24 Squadron for duty with the York flight, then at Northolt. A personal aircraft for Mr Churchill had been delivered to the squadron: this was *Ascalon*, the second prototype, LV633, luxuriously equipped (for the time) with a private cabin and toilet, a dining saloon-cum-conference room seating eight, and eight further sleeper-style bunks forward of the galley. For the first time on long-range flights, the PM was to have an all-RAF crew. It was captained by Wing Commander H.B. Collins, the CO of 24 – an ex-Imperial Airways Captain of some considerable experience. I was the navigator.

After completion of its clearance trials at Boscombe Down, the York had made its maiden flight in May 1943 – a rendezvous at Gibraltar with the Boeing Clipper flying-boat bringing Mr Churchill's party from the TRIDENT Conference in Washington. After visiting Algiers and Tunis and inspecting the Mareth Line from the air, we returned to Northolt on 5 June. Mr Churchill commented to the Captain at the time, 'You will be wanted shortly for a very important passenger.' Who could be more important than the PM himself? A few days later, the presence of Group Captain 'Mouse' Fielden inspecting *Ascalon* brought back my Benson memories.

On the evening of 11 June the arrival of Guardsmen batmen with luggage in Palace cars dispelled any doubt in our minds about the identity of 'General Lyon'. At flight briefing, the AOC-in-C of Transport Command (Ginger Bowhill) addressed a few words to us about the historic occasion.

The aircraft was routed out of the UK via Lundy Island and a position 49N 10W and thence southwards, a roundabout route to keep beyond the likely range of Ju 88 night-fighters operating from the Brest Peninsula. The flight went smoothly but the landing forecast for Gibraltar was fog and, along with all other aircraft destined for the Rock, a diversion was ordered to the RAF staging post at Ras el Ma (Fez). For security reasons we had been allocated a call-sign within the block of ferry aircraft that night from the UK to North Africa – the Royal flight call-sign to be used only in dire emergency. Thus Ras el Ma had no reasons to differentiate between us and other aircraft. By chance, the direct secure link between Gibraltar and Ras el Ma was temporarily out of action. Guarded RT messages got no reception and so we took our turn in the circuit and found ourselves parked alongside an Albermarle whose crew and passengers' appearance caused some Royal comment. Their embarrassment was in no way matched by the unfortunate Station Commander's, who was woken with the news of the Royal arrival, having had a somewhat hectic Mess party the night before. We continued on to Algiers (Maison Elanche) an hour later, after refuelling and revictualling passengers, crew and aircraft.

After two days at General Eisenhower's Supreme Headquarters in Algiers, HM flew to Oran to review the US Fifth Army under General Mark Clark, on the La Senia airfield: this was but an hour and a half's flight in each direction.

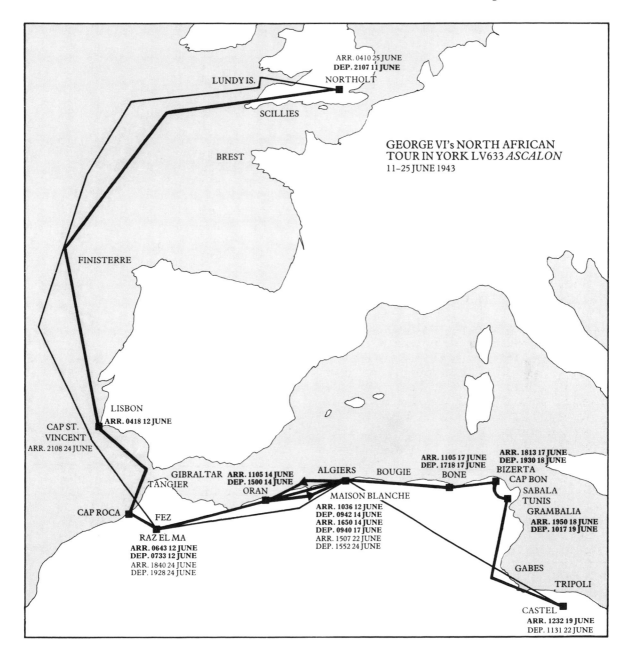

GEORGE VI's NORTH AFRICAN
TOUR IN YORK LV633 *ASCALON*
11–25 JUNE 1943

Whilst HM and his party were on the saluting-base watching the march-past, a stray US Colonel approached the York − with the inevitable camera. The crew, who were at ease in the shade of the wing, were asked, 'Say, fellows, who's the big shot?' On being told that it was HM The King, the Colonel thought for a bit and then exclaimed, 'Gee, I guess that makes you all dooks and oils.' We humbly explained that such honours and dignities had not yet been conferred upon us and he went on his way somewhat disappointed. He might have been pleased to know that on the morning we returned to the UK, we were summoned to the Palace where HM made all the flight-deck crew MVOs (4th Class), now LVO.

On 17th June, HM's tour of British Army units took him to Bone and Tunis, and two days later on to Tripoli, where he embarked in the cruiser HMS *Aurora* to visit the garrison in Malta. On his return to Tripoli he reviewed representative units of the Eighth Army before flying back to Algiers.

The homeward journey started on 24 June and we again staged at Ras el Ma to avoid any risk of fog at Gibraltar − this time with adequate warning. A wide Atlantic track was flown, similar to outbound, with Royal Navy ships on station at the major turning-points, listening on the guard frequency for any mishap. The flight was uneventful but for a much stronger tail-wind component than had been forecast. By five hours out it was clear that we were very much ahead of schedule. Speed was reduced, but the Air Equerry came forward to enquire the reason for the change in engine settings. After explanations, he ordered the Captain to resume normal cruising speed: HM had no wish to be in the air longer than necessary, as there was always a risk of interception as we neared UK, even over London. We landed at Northolt nearly an hour early but fortunately our adjusted ETAs were being passed by Ferry Control at Gloucester to the AOC-in-C, so that he and the Chief of the Air Staff were on hand. Mr Churchill, arriving a little later, found the Royal party already taking coffee in the Officers' Mess.

Just a year later, the PM let it be known that he was lending His Majesty 'his'

Avro York LV633 Ascalon, the third prototype, taking off from a strip in Italy. It was used by Winston Churchill on many of his famous overseas visits and by King George VI for his 1943 North Africa and 1944 Italy tours.

aircraft again, forgetting perhaps that all RAF aircraft belong to the Crown. This time Rabat Salé was chosen instead of Gibraltar as the intermediate staging-post. It was an all-RAF airfield with good met facilities and good approaches. Most important from a security point of view, it had the great advantage that it was not overlooked by the Duty Spy at La Linea.

Our crew was the same and we were joined, of course, by the Air Equerry, Group Captain Fielden, temporarily spared from commanding RAF Tempsford. We left Northolt at 23.10 on 22 July, slightly late closing doors as a doodlebug (V1) flew right over the airfield, fortunately without stopping. The Royal Party, which included HM Queen Elizabeth and the Princess Elizabeth, were inspecting the interior of the aircraft and there was not an air-raid shelter within a hundred yards!

Weather was good for the eight-hour flight; a PAMPAS recce had been made by Mosquito in the afternoon as far as Finisterre to check on cloud-tops, so for once met had been confident in their forecast. Two hours later, the flight was continued to Pomigliano (Naples), the RAF staging-post for the Headquarters at Caserta. This was a rather bumpy trip over lunchtime, across a typical Mediterranean cold frontal situation. The York was to remain at Pomigliano, being too large for forward airfields and too demanding in fuel to operate further north, while HM continued to the forward areas in General 'Jumbo' Wilson's Dakota (FZ631) named *Freedom* and flown by Squadron Leader Penfold. Ten days later the York was standing ready for departure to the UK via Rabat, but was delayed on take-off by an unusual Naval manoeuvre: HM was being hosted by C-in-C Med., whose driver got lost on the rather tortuous route through the back streets of Naples, selected for security reasons to keep away from the main boulevards. Land navigation had proved too much, and some Naval expletives were said to have been used.

Homeward, the weather on the Atlantic leg did produce a few bumps in the tops of cloud. Before turning in, HM came forward to appraise the flight-deck. That he knew his star recognition was evident from the interest he took in our navigation methods and progress. As we landed at Northolt on time, yet another doodlebug made its appearance.

It is interesting to compare our wartime operations with present-day practices. The aircraft was new to the service at the time, but based on the wings, tail empennage and undercarriage of the well-proven Lancaster. As to the engines, Rolls-Royce had not only their name at stake but a strong commercial interest in the performance of the aircraft in hot weather. Thus we had a permanent Rolls representative at Northolt and direct access to Derby at all times.

Planning was the same as for the PM's flights and we were fortunate that in our relationship with No. 10 we dealt through the SASO of Transport Command, Air Vice-Marshal H.G. Brackley, formerly of Imperial Airways and widely experienced over the Atlantic and Empire routes. As the intermediary between the requirements of the Palace and No. 10 (via the Chief of the Air Staff) and the Captain of aircraft, his knowledge and judgement saved us from a lot of petty interference by well-meaning but often ignorant staff officers at various levels anxious to be in on the act.

Minimum need-to-know was the rule but with the added handicap that but for established RAF bases, we could not be sure of what facilities we should find on arrival: there could be little in the way of pre-flight reconnaissance. With HM's flights, at least we were sure of the itinerary , but this was not always true of the PM's, for whom we had to make adequate provision for victualling as well as for the more mundane matters of navigation and fuel: there were little problems like keeping the bed-linen aired in Russia and the refrigerator running in Tunis!

When The King's Flight re-formed early in 1946, its first Commanding Officer was New Zealander Wing Commander Bill Tacon DSO, DFC, AFC (now Air Commodore E.W. Tacon CBE, DSO, LVO, DFC, AFC). He recalls some of the problems he faced in re-establishing the unit:

When I arrived at RAF Benson on 12 June 1946, I found that the news of the impending arrival of four aircraft, twenty officers and one hundred and twenty airmen was unwelcome news to the Station Commander, particularly as it was not known under whose command we would be operating. We were allocated the hangar which was then in use for the second-line servicing of the PRU Mosquitos, and was the filthiest hangar on the station. Squadron Leader George Pearson, the Engineering Officer, arrived at around this time and it wasn't long before we had sorted out the various offices, crew-rooms, storage space etc – but we were then faced with the awful problem of getting the hangar and offices clean. The hangar-floor was covered in oil and grease and the offices were far from satisfactory.

George and I discussed the problem and I suggested that the quickest way would be to use petrol on the floors. Provided we took a few precautions, it should work. I really admired the way George went about the job: he opened

Photographed in 1948, the Captain of The King's Flight, Air Commodore E.H. Fielden (left), with the Flight's Commanding Officer, Wing Commander E.W. Tacon.

*The King's Vickers Viking C2
VL246 was crewed in 1946 by:
Wing Commander E.W.
Tacon DSO, DFC, AFC, pilot;
Flight Lieutenant A.J. Lee, co-
pilot; Flight Lieutenant D.
Fowkes, navigator; and Flight
Lieutenant L.G.S. Reed DFC,
signals.*

*The King's Flight's fourth
Viking, VL248, was the
freighter/workshop aircraft
and was crewed in 1946 by:
Flight Lieutenant R.J.
Harrison, pilot; Flight
Lieutenant E.B. Trubshaw,
co-pilot; Flight Lieutenant
W.E. Boteler DFC, navigator;
and Flight Lieutenant F.
Myers AFC, signals. The third
Viking C2, VL245, served as
the Royal Household and
groundcrew aircraft, crewed by
Flight Lieutenants W.E.
Welch, A.E. Richmond, A.P.
O'Hara DFC, DFM, and P.H.
McKenna DFM. VL245 was
the first of the special Vikings
to arrive at The King's Flight
as it required least
modification, while VL248
was the last, as it required most
work. VL245, following an
accident in 1947, was replaced
by two standard Viking C1s,
VL232 and VL233.*

*Members of The King's
Flight's aircrews pose in front
of The Queen's Viking.*

both ends of the hangar, stationed men on all approaches to the hangar to keep away unwanted intruders, had a line of airmen across the width of the floor with bass brooms, then brought up the petrol bowser which poured petrol over the floor as the men scrubbed with the brooms. As they reached the other end of the hangar, more men came in with high-pressure fire hoses and washed away the sludge. Some hours later, George and I heaved a great sigh of relief that not only had nothing gone wrong but that we also had a clean hangar, and after a few days with paint-brushes, the place was really transformed.

Some weeks later, there was a complaint from the local water conservancy council in Wallingford about oil and petrol in the river flowing through the town. We admitted to an oil-spill, apologised and assured them it was not likely to happen again. That was the Flight off to a clean start.

Bill Tacon had just eight months to prepare the Flight and its new Vickers Vikings for the Royal Tour of South Africa in 1947:

The first time The King flew in South Africa was on 8 March 1947 from Bloemfontein to Bulfontein and return, along with Princess Margaret. On the return flight he sat in the co-pilot's seat and, I suppose to make conversation, said to me, 'I believe this is a very safe aircraft and can fly very well on one engine,' to which I replied, 'If, sir, you look out to your right, you'll see that the starboard engine is feathered and we are flying on one engine.' I don't know how impressed he was – but I know 'Mouse' Fielden wasn't, and I received a right royal blast from him about endangering the life of the Monarch.

During the Royal Tour we had to return to the UK urgently on Palace business; my crew and I left Cape Town on 25 April 1947 and arrived in

The four original Royal Vikings on tour in South Africa in 1946.

King George VI and Princess Margaret arriving in Viking VL246 at Salisbury, Southern Rhodesia (Zimbabwe) on 7 April 1947.

Travelling together in the second Viking, Queen Elizabeth and Princess Elizabeth arriving at Salisbury on 7 April 1947, with The King greeting them at the foot of the steps. The complex logistics involved in operating four aircraft to the exacting standards and timings of The King's Flight in fairly primitive aviation conditions and in an arduous climate can readily be imagined.

Benson 32 hours 30 minutes later on 26 April. What all the hurry was about I don't recall, but it certainly proved that The King's aeroplane, VL246, was a reliable machine and that it was possible to fly 65 hours 50 minutes in four days.

On 30 March 1948, my crew and I, with 'Mouse' Fielden in the co-pilot's seat, set off for Australasia and New Zealand on a proving flight for the planned Royal Tour (later to be cancelled because of His Majesty's ill-health). The autopilot failed after we left Malta and the whole trip was flown manually. We arrived in Auckland, New Zealand, on 6 April, having flown 50 hours 50 minutes in seven days. After visiting fifteen airfields in New Zealand and discussing tour arrangements, we left for Canberra. In Australia we visited some forty-four airfields before setting off for the UK from Perth, Western Australia on 6 May. Arriving back at Benson on 13 May, we had flown some 311 hours 25 minutes in six weeks – and no autopilot except for the first seven hours.

With Bill Tacon on the tour of South Africa was Flight Lieutenant Brian Trubshaw, who went on to achieve great distinction as Chief Test Pilot and Divisional Director, Filton, for British Aerospace. He it was who first flew the British-assembled Concorde, but appropriately, he has recorded that he was originally bitten by the flying bug when, at the age of eight, he saw the Prince of Wales' aircraft – probably one of the Gipsy Moths or Puss Moths – land on the beach at Pembrey in South Wales. He remembers the eventful years that he served with the flight:

I joined The King's Flight in the middle of 1946. I remember being interviewed in the Air Ministry by Air Commodore (as he was then) Fielden,

The King's, The Queen's and the Royal Household Vikings on tour in South Africa in 1947. The workshop Viking also went on the tour. On extended tours several aircraft were required to provide the necessary accommodation and the maintenance and repair support. The King and Princess Elizabeth (the heir to the Throne) flew in different aircraft in case of mishap.

VL247, The Queen's Viking, seen in flight.

who selected eight pilots. The four senior ones were made the captains of the four Viking aircraft which were going to be the equipment for the Royal Tour of South Africa scheduled for 1947. I, being one of the junior ones, was therefore a co-pilot and assigned to the No. 4 aeroplane, which was fitted out as a workshop.

The early days we spent training vigorously on the Viking, which was not a particularly nice aeroplane from some points of view, although it did pretty noble service in the Flight over the years. We did run into some engine-surging troubles on one of the first proving flights during a take-off from Nairobi. That was quite an exercise, because the aeroplane really paddled down the runway from side to side as each engine surged in turn. That problem was eventually fixed, but only just in time for the tour of South Africa to take place.

Also during this initial build-up period, we did a bit of flying around the UK in the Dominie (RL951) and in fact I was in the Dominie on the night of 11 November 1946 when it ran out of fuel over Oxford and we came down in a field near Mount Farm. The accident smashed the aeroplane to pieces, but none of the individuals on board had even one scratch. I was actually sitting in the back of the aeroplane when I found the navigator sitting on my feet and said to him, 'What the hell are you doing down there?' whereupon he said, 'We're about to crash!' So I came out of my slumbers and began to take a little bit of interest, and I also realised that it was kind of quiet outside because neither of the engines was running.

We got back into the Mess after the accident and there was the Benson 'gen' man called Pudsey, a Mosquito pilot, sitting at the bar, which was in the hall in those days. Pudsey said to me, 'I don't like the sound of this. Meet me at the back of the Mess in fifteen minutes.'

Five captains who flew The King's Flight's Vikings in 1948. From left to right: Flight Lieutenant S.N. Sloan DFC, CGM, staff aircraft No. 2; Flight Lieutenant E.B. Trubshaw, the workshop/freighter; Squadron Leader H.A. Nash AFC, The King's aircraft; Squadron Leader R.H.F. Payne MVO, AFC, The Queen's aircraft; and Flight Lieutenant A.J. Lee, staff aircraft No. 1.

The Queen and the Duke of Edinburgh disembark from a Royal Viking.

Still being a little bit shaken, I went out to see what Pudsey was up to and found that he was loading petrol cans, ropes, axes and all sorts of stuff into his car. 'What are you going to do?' I asked.

He replied, 'We're going out to burn it.'

We set off on this venture in Pudsey's car, but by the time we got to the wreckage, there were a couple of rather nasty Alsatians walking around it with their Corporal handlers, so we just retired to the George in Dorchester and finished the evening there.

Then the Tour came off, and off we went to South Africa. The No. 4 aeroplane brought up the rear and when we got as far as Tabora (it took the workshop, as it was called, some time – you couldn't put much fuel in it,

Flight Lieutenant A.J. Lee and Flight Lieutenant E.B. Trubshaw (right), The King's Flight's first two helicopter pilots, trained ab initio *for the task, conversing in front of one of the Flight's Hoverflies.*

because it was carrying all those spare parts), we found the No. 1 aeroplane, that was with 'Mouse' Fielden and Bill Tacon, waiting for us and in need of a new gill motor, necessary for the air-cooling of the engine. I immediately went into the great book of words to see which rack this would be located in and was somewhat horrified to find that we didn't have a gill motor on board. Those who knew 'Mouse' Fielden will well appreciate that he was very far from pleased.

The tour itself was uneventful. We spent most of the time based in Cape Town, but we moved both to Pretoria and to Rhodesia as it then was, when the Royal party moved to those areas. After a most enjoyable tour and our return to England, the Flight was cut into two, but I was one of the lucky ones who was kept on.

We immediately started on another venture as part of selling air transportation to the Royal Family: it was decided that the mail would be delivered to Balmoral by helicopter. The two junior people, of which I was one as there were now only four pilots left in the Flight, were taught how to fly helicopters for this particular purpose. This was an amazing experience because we used the old Hoverfly Mk I which was made by Sikorsky. Its cruising speed and maximum speed was sixty miles an hour, so it took us some thirteen hours to fly these two things up to Aberdeen from Benson.

We started the mail run by driving over to Balmoral on the first day to have a look at the cricket ground which was going to be our landing-strip; in fact we were honoured to have lunch with the Royal Family and then were sent back to Aberdeen to fetch the helicopters. We brought them over and all the younger members of the Royal Family jumped in and out of them all afternoon, having a good look at them. I remember a very embarrassing experience when the late Prince William of Gloucester, on getting out of my helicopter, put his hand on the hot exhaust – he let out a bellow which could be heard all round the high ground north of Balmoral and I should think that the echo could have travelled even further. The burn was not too bad, I am glad to say, and with a little tenderness from his mother all was quickly restored.

We then started the mail runs proper and on the first morning were met by the Court Postmaster – who used to get extremely upset if he was only called 'the Postmaster'. He took us both to the senior servants' hall for breakfast, where we had a very hearty occasion. When we got back to Aberdeen, though, I had a call from Sir Harold Campbell, who was the Equerry in Waiting at the time, to say that The Queen was very upset that we had been taken to the senior servants' hall; of course we must have breakfast, but in future it would be in the dining room. The other pilot, Alan Lee, and I were a little bit nervous about this and were rather shy in asking for the toast to be passed. But it was a most amusing time – we went to the Ghillies' Ball and found ourselves doing all sorts of dances unfamiliar to us. Finally in that summer of 1947, we had a dinner party at Balmoral given for the two of us and that was really a very memorable occasion.

In the summer of 1948 we started up again on the mail run to Balmoral, but this time we did it quite differently in that we were working up to the Royal Tour of Australia and New Zealand scheduled for the autumn of 1948, so we were not actually based at Aberdeen in quite the same manner as we had been in 1947. With the cancellation of that Royal Tour, those of us who had been on the Flight since its re-formation in 1946 were obviously time-expired on our duty period, and were posted elsewhere. I still managed to keep in touch with the Flight, though, because 'Mouse' Fielden in fact got me my job as a Test

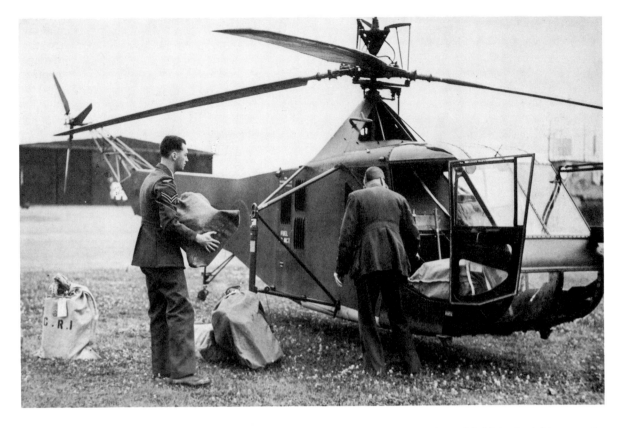

Mail being loaded into one of The King's Flight's Hoverflies at Dyce for Balmoral. The use of what was still in many respects an experimental form of aviation was an imaginative move characteristic of The King's Flight keeping pace with aviation.

A King's Flight Hoverfly in flight over Deeside. Helicopters were ideally suited to the terrain, where fixed-wing aircraft could not operate and road links were slow.

Pilot with Vickers Armstrong. Without his guidance I would certainly never have gone into the aircraft industry, so I owe him a particular debt as far as my future life has worked out. When I went to Vickers, we still used to have the Vikings back from the Flight for their major servicings and it was my privilege to do the test flying on them and then deliver them back to Benson, so contact was maintained for a great many years.

The reader will have gathered that Sir Edward Fielden was the dominating figure of the Flight during the thirty-three years that he was associated with it. Wing Commander Bussey came to know him well:

I believe all who knew Sir Edward well would agree he was a man for minute detail, detested incompetence, was witty at times, short on temper and tight with his money.

I remember one flight in the Hudson from Dumfries to Wittering with the Duke and Duchess of Gloucester on board, early in the war. All Hudson flights were planned precisely, the flight-plan being drawn distinctly on maps neatly folded for convenience of the pilot. These were numbered in order of requirement during the flight and held by the radio operator in readiness. They were handed to the Captain on the order of 'Next'.

On this particular flight, we experienced very poor visibility and rough conditions en route for our pin-point, Rhyl on the Welsh coast. I was occupying the right-hand seat and was aware of the tense atmosphere caused by the knowledge that the Liverpool balloon barrage was not far away to port. I saw only fleeting glimpses of the sea. At our ETA Rhyl, the Captain uttered 'Next'. The map was passed forward, but the wrong one! The Captain took a brief look and hurled the map over his shoulder towards the radio operator. Unfortunately the cabin door was open and the map flew into the saloon and ended on the feet of the Duchess.

Whilst the maps were being sorted out, the Captain indicated that I should go and recover the lost map; immediately on my return I had the good fortune to see Rhyl below. When I reported this, the Captain said, 'I suppose the Duchess pointed it out to you.' We landed at Wittering on schedule.

I mentioned in my previous contribution to this chapter that the Navy shot at us a couple of times. The sequel came months later: in his office, the Captain said, 'I saw one of the Sea Lords the other day and told him about his chaps shooting at us. He was quite upset.'

'I think he should be, having shot at the Royal Aircraft,' I said.

'It's not that,' the Captain replied. 'He was angry because they did not hit us.'

After the war the Captain acquired a farm at Pangbourne, and on my first visit I saw a very elderly, arthritic-looking gander. 'He came with the farm', I was told. Many years later, Sir Edward suggested he donate a goose to our Christmas draw (he did not normally make a donation) and on receipt, I recognised this as the elderly gander. One of our technicians won it, and a few weeks later was off sick, having all his teeth extracted. When I reported this, the Captain commented, 'I knew it was a good bird but not that good.'

The Captain purchased four Muscovy ducks and a drake from an RAF station farm in Yorkshire. These were crated and placed in the aircraft hold, along with some household baggage. Unfortunately, the baggage-handlers at London airport off-loaded the ducks with the baggage, to the consternation of all concerned. The Captain had no time for baggage-handlers and commented, 'Typical – they don't know birds from baggage.'

He was hoping to build up a nice stock from these birds and frequently gave progress reports on their egg-laying and the number of eggs he had in the incubator and under hens. It was a major tragedy when not a single egg hatched out. He reported his failure to the supplier of the birds, and during their discussion he realised that the supplier was a Group Captain with whom he had had a difference of opinion during the war. He commented, 'That chap had that blasted drake sterilised before he sold him to me. I suppose we are quits now.' That Group Captain was the only man that I know who appeared to have got the better of the Captain in a deal.

'We're off to the Palace,' the Captain said one morning. 'Top secret job. I want you to pick up the Queen Mother's Land-Rover from the Mews, put it in a Hastings at Abingdon, go with it to Aldergrove and hand it intact to the Army. Tell no-one about it.'

I picked up the vehicle and insisted I had an identity note from the Controller of the Mews as the vehicle had no registration plates. The vehicle was completely open, it was a lovely day and I got on fine until a conscientious young police constable stopped me in Maidenhead. I proved my identity but he did not believe me and I found myself trying to get the Inspector to check with the Mews. He would not, and it took some half-hour or so to clear me through the London police. I delivered the vehicle and reported the incident to the Captain. His comment was: 'Well, you were wearing your beret. You would have been all right if you had on your peaked cap!' Some sympathy I got!

Back on his Pangbourne farm, the Captain had acquired some special black sheep from one of the Scottish Isles, and had great hopes of building up a flock. At lambing, the first arrival was taken by a fox, so he decided he would attempt to shoot the culprit the following night. He sat in the hedge in the corner of the field, watching his sheep by the light of a full moon. He saw a flash of white in the hedge opposite and 'I gave him my right,' he grunted, 'and I gave him my left.' He was surprised indeed when a man rose pleading 'Don't shoot' from the spot! His neighbour was on a similar mission and the white flash the Captain had mistaken for the fox was in fact his bald head. The Captain said, 'I thought I should take him to hospital, although I don't much care for the chap.'

The incident made front-page headlines – 'Queen's Equerry Shoots Neighbour'. Some few days later we were in Nigeria, preparing for a Royal visit, when the Captain produced a telegram he had just received from his friend, the Governor of Tanganyika, who has just received his *Daily Express*. It read something like this: 'Have just seen the *Daily Express*. Good shooting. Bad luck. God Save The Queen.'

Africa seems to have been an eventful area for the Flight, and reference has already been made on page 56 to the arrest of Wing Commander Attlee's Heron in Mali in 1961. Now Air Vice-Marshal D.L. Attlee CBE, LVO, recounts the incident in his own words:

I suppose my suspicions that all was not as it should have been were first aroused when the controller failed to answer the initial call for landing instructions, for we were expected and well within range. The crew and I had been very well entertained the previous evening by the French Commandant of the Beau Geste-type Algerian oasis of El Golea. We had taken off at sunrise for In Salah, another, smaller watering and refuelling place in the middle of the Algerian desert. Now, at midday on Sunday 9 July 1961, we were at 9,000 feet

Character is etched into the face in this portrait of the man who in so many ways epitomised the spirit of The King's Flight and The Queen's Flight, Air Vice-Marshal Sir Edward Fielden GCVO, CB, DFC, AFC. It provides a fascinating comparison with the portrait of the fresh-faced young officer on page 70. Fielden was the Captain of The King's Flight from July 1936 to February 1942 and again, upon its re-formation, from May 1946 to July 1952, and Captain of The Queen's Flight from August 1952 until retiring in January 1962, but he remained keenly involved in the Flight as a Senior Air Equerry to HM The Queen from 1 January 1962 to 31 December 1969.

approaching Gao, a town on the banks of the Niger and some 200 miles east of Timbuktu.

Gao was not a planned refuelling stop on the route to Accra. It had been substituted for Tessalit only thirty-six hours before leaving England at the insistence of the Air Attaché in Paris. He had assured us that Tessalit had just been abandoned by the French and there was no fuel available. Both Tessalit and Gao are in the Republic of Mali, a former French African colonial territory, and there should have been little difficulty over changing airfields within the same country. So I was surprised, when we eventually made radio contact, to be asked if we had authority to land. I knew we had, but without a piece of paper it was going to be difficult to prove. And we certainly had not got the authority to land anywhere else, even if we had the fuel to get there.

I was certain that we had a small problem on our hands when we taxied in. I had never before been marshalled to a parking-place by a number of natives inexpertly waving Tommy-guns and rifles. I was also a little perturbed to see a small crowd of Europeans apparently behind a barbed-wire fence.

What appeared to be a company of fully-armed Mali police surrounded the aircraft and, when we got out, they inevitably asked for the authority to land. A lengthy explanation then took place, which became more and more one-sided since it was conducted entirely in French, a language in which none of us was proficient. It became evident that the aircraft was not to be moved or refuelled, but it was quite impossible to discover a way round the impasse. The situation was not made much easier by the arrival from behind the wire of a number of French army and air force officers, none of whom could speak a word of English. One explained that even French aircraft had to have written authority for every landing, which was apparently only obtainable from Bamako, the capital of Mali and about 600 miles to the west. And it was Sunday.

The first hopeful sign was the arrival of a police Lieutenant. Up to now the police had been 'controlled' by an enormous and very dim Sergeant. Now he and his men fell silent, while the Lieutenant had the story told to him in our halting French. He was prepared to be sympathetic and thought the incident could be forgotten, but some of his men took him to one side and changed his mind for him. However, he did allow the aircraft to be taxied to the refuelling point, although one of the crew had to remain with him as a 'hostage'. At the same time, barrels were being placed along the taxiway and runway to prevent an unauthorised departure.

While the refuelling was being carried out with the assistance of French air force personnel, another member of the crew, whose French was the least basic, was driven into the town of Gao, some five miles away, to see the Governor of the Province. During more lengthy explanations, still in French, the Governor showed that he knew quite well what the aircraft was doing, where it was going and why. But it appeared that he had not the authority to release it, and he would have to cable his government in Bamako for instructions. Furthermore, he forbade the crew to send a message to the British Ambassador in Bamako. And it was Sunday.

Back at the airfield, the French Commandant had arrived and at last I thought we should get some sense out of someone. But it transpired that the French had practically no influence with the Mali officials; not only were they unwelcome guests, but they were leaving in three weeks for good. The wire had been put up not so much to keep the French in, as the Malis out. The Commandant was prepared to, and did, put every facility under his control at our disposal, but he was extraordinarily reluctant even to talk to the local provincial Governor. He did eventually phone, but his arguments made no impression at all. He also agreed to send a signal to Bamako over the French forces network, but I am sure that this would not have been done if I had mentioned that the Governor had banned all cables to the capital.

The aircraft now had to be locked up in a hangar pending further instructions. This meant starting the engines, which also supplied power to the HF radio. The opportunity was too good to miss. With luck, we should be able to talk to Accra direct, but the distance to the hangar was only about fifty yards, which did not allow much time. By some most inefficient taxying the distance was slightly increased but, although Accra could hear us, they could not understand the message. However, the French operator at Niamey did and, efficient as ever, undertook to relay the message. Subsequently, we learnt that the punch was lost, as we had used the word 'arrested'. When this was relayed by a Frenchman, it came out as 'stopped'. In Ghana, they knew we were 'stopping' at Gao and took no notice. And anyway, it was Sunday.

After parking the aircraft, the crew were ordered into an ancient French bus and taken to the hotel in Gao. This was, I think, called the 'Splendide'. Outwardly, it might once have lived up to its name, with Automobile Association Afrique and International Tourist signs still hanging outside, though why anyone should want to spend a night in Gao, I cannot imagine. Inside, the hotel was anything but 'splendide'. It had been shut for three months, there was nothing to eat or drink and it was indescribably filthy. We quickly decided that this was no place for a night-stop and demanded to be returned to the French officers' mess. The wrangling and argument with and between Mali officials over this one simple point lasted for four hours.

During the discussion, we were approached by a Mali who was slightly better dressed than his compatriots — he even wore a tie — and who introduced

Heron C4 XM295 (illustrated) and XM296 were handed over by the manufacturer to The Queen's Flight on 16 April 1958. The Flight's fourth Heron, C4 XR391, was handed over on 16 June 1961. It was XM296 which was arrested in Mali in 1961.

himself as Georges Segou. His suggestion that we might like a beer was the most constructive remark any Mali had yet made. Leaving the debating Malis, Georges led us for about a hundred yards along the banks of the Niger, where a flock of naked children were splashing in the muddy and sluggish water, to an adobe house which also did duty as the local bistro. The beer was a well-known French brand. It came out of a fridge which worked, and cost the equivalent of ten shillings a bottle. Since we were guests, we thought it would be impolite to offer to buy a round too early.

Over the first glass, we discovered that Georges' French was even worse than ours and his English, of which he claimed some knowledge, bore no resemblance to any language yet heard. In fact, his invitation to drinks was about the only intelligible phrase he knew and it was obviously well-rehearsed. It was therefore not before the second beer that we realised that Georges must be some sort of 'commissar', and that he was trying to obtain a 'confession' from us. Through some very elementary French, a few words of English and some complicated signs, he indicated that we should trust and confide in him. He said he was anti-Communist, anti-French, pro-British and pro-Russian. He was not certain about America. We interrupted this line of conversation, before it passed the bounds of credibility, by suggesting another beer. Georges promptly ordered whisky and continued by asking whether we could fly him to France, or anywhere as long as it was out of Mali and not into Ghana.

Georges was becoming something of a bore, and a most tenacious one. He followed us back to the hotel, where the same Malis, aided by some other disinterested parties, were still arguing the next move. Fortified by the beer, our French more fluent though less accurate, we singled out the most influential-looking Mali and again demanded a car to take us back to the airfield. Strangely, and in spite of Georges' protestations, it arrived within an hour; accompanied as far as the gates by Georges, we returned to an excellent dinner and comfortable beds in clean rooms. Shortly after midnight, the French duty officer told us that we were free to go, and at seven the next morning we took off for Accra.

I returned to Gao some five months later in a similar aircraft. The French had gone but the same Malis were there, all smiles and co-operation. Of Georges there was no sign. We refuelled in twenty minutes and were off. All was in order. And it was not Sunday.

APPENDIX 1. ROYAL AIRCRAFT

Dates	Serial No. (*Aircraft of The King's Flight and The Queen's Flight)	Type	Remarks
1919	C4451	Avro 504J	Flying instruction for Prince Albert.
Apr 28 – Oct 28	J8430	Bristol Fighter	No. 24 Sqn.
Jun 28 – 1930	J9095	Westland Wapiti 1A	No. 24 Sqn.
Sep 29 – 4 Feb 33	G-AALG	de Havilland DH60M Gipsy Moth	Owned by the Prince of Wales. Sold to Miss Jean Batten.
1930	K1115	Fairey 111F	No. 24 Sqn.
16 Jul 30 – 18 Jul 30	G-ABCW	de Havilland DH60M Gipsy Moth	Owned by the Prince of Wales. Written off in accident.
1930	J9772	Hawker Tomtit	No. 24 Sqn. Prince of Wales visit to Dover.
1930	G-AALL	Hawker Tomtit	On loan by Hawker to No. 24 Sqn. for the King's Cup Air Race.
28 Jul 30 – 19 Jan 31	G-ABBS	de Havilland DH80A Puss Moth	Owned by the Prince of Wales.
22 Aug 30 – 12 Jul 33	G-ABDB	de Havilland DH60M Gipsy Moth	Owned by the Duke of Gloucester. Part-exchanged for G-ACGG.
18 Dec 30 – Aug 31	G-ABFV	de Havilland DH80A Puss Moth	Owned by the Prince of Wales. Shipped to Brazil for 1931 tour.
11 Jul 31 – 22 Sep 31	G-ABEG	Westland Wessex	Hired by the Prince of Wales for his holiday in France.
14 Jul 31 – 19 Dec 32	G-ABNN	de Havilland DH80A Puss Moth	Owned by the Prince of Wales. Exchanged for G-ACDD.
16 Sep 31 – 24 May 33	G-ABRR	de Havilland DH80A Puss Moth	Owned by the Prince of Wales. Part-exchanged for G-ACGG.

Dates	Serial No. (*Aircraft of The King's Flight and The Queen's Flight)	Type	Remarks
19 Dec 32 – 17 Mar 33	G-ACDD	de Havilland DH83 Fox Moth	Owned by the Prince of Wales. Sold to de Havilland. Re-registered in Belgium.
5 Apr 33 – Jun 33	G-ABXS	de Havilland DH83 Fox Moth	Owned by the Prince of Wales. Part-exchanged for G-ACGG.
16 May 33 – Mar 35	G-ACCC	Vickers Viastra X	Owned by and specially built for the Prince of Wales.
12 Jun 33 – 5 Feb 35	G-ACGG	de Havilland DH84 Dragon	Owned by the Prince of Wales. Sold to R. Shuttleworth Esq.
27 Apr 35 – 13 Mar 36	G-ACTT	de Havilland DH89 Dragon Rapide	Owned by the Prince of Wales. Sold to Olley Air Services. Originally allotted to Anglo-American Oil Co Ltd.
8 Jun 35 – 8 May 37	G-ADDD	de Havilland DH89 Dragon Rapide	Owned by the Prince of Wales. Sold to Western Airways Ltd.
7 May 37 – 30 Oct 39	*G-AEXX	Airspeed Envoy	First Royal aircraft to be publicly financed. Re-allocated to No. 24 Sqn. as L7270.
9 Aug 39 – 22 Jun 42	*N7263	Lockheed Hudson (Long Range)	Re-allocated to No. 161 Sqn.
12 Feb 40 – 4 Mar 40	N7364	Lockheed Hudson	Loaned to The King's Flight by No. 24 Sqn. Re-allocated to PDU Heston.
15 Mar 40 – 25 May 42	*P5634	Percival Q6	Used by C-in-C Bomber Command. Re-allocated to Halton.
7 Sep 40 – 14 Feb 41	*G-AGCC	de Havilland DH95 Flamingo	Re-allocated to No. 24 Sqn. as R2766.
1 Jan 40 – 19 Apr 42	*K6120	Avro Tutor	Crashed en route to Silloth 19 Apr 42.
6 Jun 45 – Dec 45	KN386	Douglas Dakota IV	No. 24 Sqn. Reverted to general VIP work.
15 Jul 46 – 11 Nov 46	*RL951	de Havilland Dominie	Written off in forced landing.
11 Aug 46 – Jul 48	*VL245	Vickers Viking C2	Staff aircraft. Crashed at Aberdeen 12 Sep 47.
4 Oct 46 – 6 Feb 47	VL226	Vickers Viking C1A	On loan – returned to Vickers. The first Viking.
27 Dec 46 – 6 Feb 47	VL227	Vickers Viking C1A	On loan – returned to Vickers. Originally G-AIKN. The second Viking.
12 Jan 47 – 30 Apr 58	*VL246	Vickers Viking C2	The King's aeroplane. Sold to Tradair.
Jan 47 – 29 Apr 58	*VL247	Vickers Viking C2	The Queen's aeroplane. Sold to Tradair.
Jan 47 – Nov 53	*VL248	Vickers Viking C2	Workshop aircraft. Sold in Mexico.
6 Aug 47 – 30 Sep 47	KL110	Sikorsky Hoverfly 1	On loan from RN for mail delivery to Balmoral. Returned to Brize Norton. Initially delivered to Canada. Was one of a series of 45, KK969 to KL113.

Dates	Serial No. (*Aircraft of The King's Flight and The Queen's Flight)	Type	Remarks
8 Aug 47 – 16 Aug 47	KL106	Sikorsky Hoverfly 1	On loan from RN for mail delivery to Balmoral. Abandoned at Aberdeen after engine failure.
25 Aug 47 – 30 Sep 47	KK973	Sikorsky Hoverfly 1	On loan from RN for mail delivery to Balmoral. Returned to Feltham.
10 Jan 48 – 24 Feb 48	MW140	Avro York	On loan for flight to Ceylon. Returned to Bassingbourn. One of 200 Avro 685 York C1's of which MW100-102 were the VIPs.
5 Jul 48 – Oct 48	KL110	Sikorsky Hoverfly 1	On loan from RN for mail delivery to Balmoral.
6 Jul 48 – 30 Apr 58	*VL233	Vickers Viking C2	Sold to Tradair.
10 Jul 48 – Aug 48	KK987	Sikorsky Hoverfly 1	On loan from RN for mail delivery to Balmoral.
21 Jul 48 – 5 Apr 57	*VL232	Vickers Viking C2	Sold to British Eagle.
29 Jul 48 – Oct 48	KL104	Sikorsky Hoverfly 1	On loan from RN for mail delivery to Balmoral.
29 Oct 52 – 18 Apr 53	WP861	de Havilland Chipmunk T10	Prince Philip's flying instruction at White Waltham.
10 Dec 52 – 15 Feb 53	WP912	de Havilland Chipmunk T10	Prince Philip's flying instruction at White Waltham.
10 Feb 53 – 9 May 53	FX459	North American Harvard	Prince Philip's instruction at White Waltham.
17 Feb 53 – 27 Nov 53	KF729	North American Harvard	Prince Philip's instruction at White Waltham
21 Apr 53 – 17 Jun 53	V4204	Airspeed Oxford	Prince Philip's instructional and communications flying.
9 Jun 53 – 25 Oct 60	*VP961	de Havilland Devon	Originally for Prince Philip's instructional and communications flying. Joined The Queen's Flight Jul 55. Re-allocated to 27MU Shawbury.
15 Jun 54 – 21 Jul 54	221	Boulton Paul Balliol	Prince Philip's flying training at White Waltham.
28 Aug 54 – 23 Apr 55	WF848	de Havilland Chipmunk T10	Prince Philip's flying training at White Waltham.
1 Sep 54 – 9 Aug 58	XF261	Westland Dragonfly HC4	On loan to The Queen's Flight from CFS (H). Returned to South Cerney.
3 Jan 55 – 27 Jan 55	460	Gloster Meteor	Prince Philip's flying instruction.
17 Jan 55 – 12 Apr 55	G-AMTS	de Havilland Heron	On loan from de Havilland for Prince Philip's use.
8 Apr 55 – 16 Apr 55	WV678	Percival Provost	Prince Philip's instruction at White Waltham.
18 May 55 – 17 Sep 64	*XH375	de Havilland Heron C3	Prince Philip's personal aeroplane. Sold to Hawker Siddeley in 1968.
31 May 56 – 7 Jun 56	XJ432	Westland Whirlwind HC2	On loan to The Queen's Flight

Dates	Serial No. (*Aircraft of The King's Flight and The Queen's Flight)	Type	Remarks
16 Apr 58 – 12 Jan 65	*XM295	de Havilland Heron C4	Re-allocated to 27 MU Shawbury, sold to Hawker Siddeley in 1968.
16 Apr 58 – 5 Jul 68	*XM296	de Havilland Heron C4	Re-allocated to Leconfield.
24 Jul 58 – Dec 59	XL111	Westland Whirlwind HAR4	On loan to The Queen's Flight. Subsequently converted to HAR10.
1 Oct 59 – 25 May 64	*XN126	Westland Whirlwind HCC8 }	Returned to Westlands, Weston-super-Mare, for conversion to HAR10.
5 Nov 59 – 25 May 64	*XN127	Westland Whirlwind HCC8 }	
20 Sep 60 – 12 Jun 64	*WP903	de Havilland Chipmunk T10	For use by Prince Philip. Subsequently used for instructional flying for the Duke of Kent, Prince Michael and Prince William.
13 Jan 61 – Mar 61	KN452	Douglas Dakota	On loan to The Queen's Flight for State Visit to Nepal.
13 Jan 61 – Mar 61	KN645	Douglas Dakota	
16 Jun 61 – 17 Jun 68	*XR391	de Havilland Heron C4	Re-allocated to 27 MU Shawbury.
26 Mar 64 – 7 Dec 67	*XR487	Westland Whirlwind HCC12	Destroyed in fatal accident.
31 Mar 64 – 2 Jul 64	G-ARAY	Hawker Siddeley HS748	On loan from Hawker Siddeley for crew training.
6 May 64 – 23 Jul 69	*XR486	Westland Whirlwind HCC12	Re-allocated to No. 32 Sqn.
10 Jul 64 –	*XS790	Hawker Siddeley Andover CC2	
7 Aug 64 –	*XS789	Hawker Siddeley Andover CC2	
1 May 65 – 7 May 65	XS794	Hawker Siddeley Andover CC2	On loan to The Queen's Flight from Met. Comm. Sqn.
26 Jun 67 – 24 Jul 67	XS794	Hawker Siddeley Andover CC2	On loan to The Queen's Flight from Met. Comm. Sqn.
27 Jun 67 – 12 Jul 67	XT672	Westland Wessex HC2	On loan to The Queen's Flight from No. 72 Sqn.
12 Dec 67 –	*XS793	Hawker Siddeley Andover CC2	Re-allocated from No. 152 Sqn.
31 Jan 68 – Jul 69	*XP299	Westland Whirlwind HAR10	Re-allocated from No. 230 Sqn.
27 Jun 68 – 28 Jun 68	XT672	Westland Wessex HC2	On loan to The Queen's Flight from No. 72 Sqn.
Jul 68 – Aug 70	*WP903	de Havilland Chipmunk T10	Flying instruction for the Prince of Wales. Re-allocated to 27 MU Shawbury.
10 Dec 68 – 5 Aug 69	*XV726	Westland Wessex HC2	Allotted for crew training. Re-allocated to No. 72 Sqn.
25 Jun 69 –	*XV732	Westland Wessex HCC4	
27 Jun 69 – 16 Sep 71	*XS770	Beagle Basset CC1	Flying instruction for the Prince of Wales. Re-allocated to No. 32 Sqn.
11 Jul 69 –	*XV733	Westland Wessex HCC4	
17 Apr 70 – 20 Apr 70	XV725	Westland Wessex HC2	On loan to The Queen's Flight from No. 72 Sqn.
28 Jan 71 – 4 Feb 71	XS794	Hawker Siddeley Andover CC2	On loan to The Queen's Flight from Met. Comm. Sqn.
8 Mar 71 – 20 Aug 71	XW322	BAC Jet Provost T5	Flying instruction for the Prince of Wales at Cranwell.
8 Mar 71 – 20 Aug 71	XW323	BAC Jet Provost T5	Flying instruction for the Prince of Wales at Cranwell

Dates	Serial No. (*Aircraft of The King's Flight and The Queen's Flight)	Type	Remarks
29 Mar 79 – 13 Apr 79	WP904	de Havilland Chipmunk T10	Detached from RN Grading Flight for flying instruction for Prince Andrew.
21 Jul 80 – 24 Jul 80	XN151	Sedbergh Glider	Detached from ACCGS Newton for gliding instruction for Prince Edward.
9 Apr 80 – 15 Apr 80	G-ASYD	BAe 111-475	British Aerospace evaluation by Prince Philip.
10 Sep 84 – 11 Sep 84 / 13 May 85 – 18 May 85	G-BGCO	Piper Seminole	British Aerospace flying instruction for the Duke of Kent.
23 Apr 86 –	*ZE700	BAe 146 CC2	
30 June 86 –	*ZE701	BAe 146 CC2	

APPENDIX 2. SENIOR EXECUTIVES OF THE KING'S FLIGHT AND THE QUEEN'S FLIGHT

SENIOR AIR EQUERRY TO HM THE QUEEN

Air Vice-Marshal Sir Edward Fielden GCVO,
  CB, DFC, AFC   1 Jan 62   –   31 Dec 69

CAPTAINS

Air Commodore Sir Edward Fielden KCVO,
  CB, DFC, AFC   21 Jul 36 –   31 Dec 61
Air Commodore A.D. Mitchell CVO, DFC, AFC   21 Mar 62 –   1 Aug 64
Air Commodore J.H.L. Blount DFC   2 Aug 64 –   7 Dec 67
Air Commodore Sir Archie Winskill KCVO, CBE,
  DFC, AE, MRAeS   15 Feb 68 –   27 Jan 82
Air Vice-Marshal J. de M. Severne LVO, OBE, AFC   27 Jan 82 –

DEPUTY CAPTAINS

Group Captain A.D. Mitchell DFC, AFC   6 Nov 56 –   7 Oct 59
Group Captain T.N. Stack AFC   13 Jul 59 –   25 Nov 62
Group Captain J. Wallace DSO, LVO, DFC, AFC   25 Apr 60 –   5 Aug 63
Group Captain P.W.D. Heal AFC   11 Jun 62 –   28 Feb 63
Group Captain P.E. Vaughan-Fowler DSO, DFC, AFC   11 Feb 63 –   29 Dec 66
Group Captain J.L. Gilbert AFC   17 Jan 66 –   30 Jan 68
Group Captain A.R. Gordon-Cumming   28 Dec 66 –   17 Oct 69
Group Captain B.A. Primavesi   11 Mar 68 –   13 Aug 71
Group Captain R.C.F. Peirse   13 Oct 69 –   1 Feb 72
Group Captain M.A. D'Arcy   5 Aug 71 –   8 Jul 74
Group Captain B. D'Iongh   2 Feb 72 –   16 Mar 73
Group Captain D.L. Edmunds AFC, ADC   16 Mar 73 –   31 Mar 78
Group Captain J.D. Spottiswood AFC, ADC   7 Jul 74 –   5 Dec 76

Group Captain R.A. Miller OBE, ADC, MRAeS, MBIM	6 Dec 76 –	30 Nov 78
Group Captain K.J. Goodwin CBE, AFC, ADC	1 Dec 78 –	1 Dec 79
Group Captain D. St J. Homer LVO, ADC	7 May 78–	9 Jan 81
Group Captain A. Mumford OBE, ADC	12 Dec 79 –	14 Jan 83
Group Captain J.F.B. Jones ADC	9 Jan 81 –	
Group Captain R.B. Duckett AFC, ADC	14 Jan 83 –	22 Feb 85
Group Captain A.M. Wills OBE, ADC	23 Feb 85 –	

COMMANDING OFFICERS

Wing Commander E.W. Tacon DSO, DFC, AFC	1 May 46–	31 Dec 49
Wing Commander R.C.E. Scott AFC	1 Jan 50 –	28 Feb 53
Wing Commander J.E. Grindon DSO, AFC	1 Mar 53 –	9 Sep 56
Wing Commander D.F. Hyland-Smith DFC, AFC	10 Sep 56 –	31 Dec 58
Wing Commander H.G. Currell DFC, AFC	1 Jan 59 –	30 Jun 59
Wing Commander R.G. Wakeford OBE, AFC	1 Jul 59 –	1 Jan 61
Wing Commander D.L. Attlee	2 Jan 61 –	21 Jul 63
Wing Commander A.W. Ringer AFC	22 Jul 63 –	4 Feb 68
Wing Commander M.J. Rayson	5 Feb 68 –	19 May 70
Wing Commander D.M. Divers LVO	20 May 70–	31 Oct 72
Wing Commander D.W. Parsons	1 Nov 72 –	30 Nov 75
Wing Commander S. Hitchin AFC	21 Nov 75 –	6 Dec 79
Wing Commander E.T.I. King	7 Dec 79 –	17 Dec 82
Wing Commander B.P. Synnott	18 Dec 82 –	11 Oct 84
Wing Commander M.L. Schofield	12 Oct 84 –	

SENIOR ENGINEERING OFFICERS

Flight Lieutenant G.A. Pearson	1 May 46–	1 Jun 48
Flight Lieutenant W.T. Bussey BEM	1 Jun 48 –	1 Jun 50
Flight Lieutenant E.W. Lamb	1 Jun 50 –	1 Jun 52
Squadron Leader J.E. Loxton	1 Jun 52 –	12 Jan 56
Squadron Leader W.T. Bussey LVO, BEM	21 Nov 55 –	8 May 61
Squadron Leader E.W. Lamb MVO	24 Apr 61 –	16 Mar 63
Squadron Leader E.E. Lake	28 Jan 63 –	10 Sep 66
Squadron Leader A. Lloyd	10 Sep 66 –	18 Sep 67
Squadron Leader M.W. Hermon	9 Sep 67 –	7 Dec 67
Squadron Leader J. Marshall	18 Dec 67 –	12 Oct 70
Squadron Leader M.C. Darby	26 Oct 70 –	15 Mar 73
Squadron Leader J.W. Mair	18 Dec 72 –	26 Apr 76
Squadron Leader M.G. Bartlett	8 Mar 76 –	24 Mar 80
Squadron Leader C.M. Gerig	10 Mar 80 –	14 Oct 83
Squadron Leader R.C.T. Bent	15 Oct 83 –	

APPENDIX 3. FIVE HUNDRED ROYAL FLIGHTS

Squadron Leader R.M. Kerr LVO, AFC	P	H	22 Feb 60	–	1 Jul 76
*Squadron Leader R.M. Lee MVO, DFC	N	H	16 Feb 59	–	10 Oct 66
			5 Jan 68	–	31 Jan 78
Squadron Leader R.E. Mitchie LVO, MBE	N	FW	3 Jul 61	–	31 Mar 74
Squadron Leader H.G. Sealey LVO	N	FW	9 Apr 62	–	8 May 76
Squadron Leader T.A. Jackson MVO, AFC	P	FW	2 Jan 61	–	16 May 72
Squadron Leader P.G. Fearn LVO	N	FW	31 Oct 58	–	9 Aug 72
Squadron Leader J. Millar MVO, DFC	P	H	7 Jul 69	–	9 Aug 77
Sergeant R.H. Harris RVM	C	FW	1 Jun 71	–	14 Sep 77
*Squadron Leader D.J. James MVO	N	H	18 Feb 75	–	
*Squadron Leader G. Williams LVO	P	FW	1 Aug 73	–	
Squadron Leader D. Lovett LVO	P	FW	1 Mar 72	–	1 Sep 81
*Squadron Leader W.B. Sowerby MVO	N	FW	3 Jan 72	–	11 Nov 85
Squadron Leader M.J. Hawes LVO	N	FW	23 Jul 73	–	
Squadron Leader D. Hurley LVO, AFC	P	H	15 Dec 75	–	
Squadron Leader M.I.S. Anderson MVO	N	FW	1 Dec 75	–	
Squadron Leader B.J. Crawford MVO	N	H	26 Jul 77	–	
Chief Technician A. Hogan	C	H	24 Apr 76	–	
Squadron Leader D.J. Rowe LVO	P	FW	1 Apr 75	–	
Flight Lieutenant A.R. Bennett	N	H	4 Sep 78	–	20 May 85

*Aircrews who have achieved 1000 Royal flights.

P = Pilot; N = Navigator; C = Crew Chief; FW = Fixed-wing; H = Helicopters.

INDEX

ACKNOWLEDGMENTS

We wish to thank the many people whose efforts and assistance over several years brought together much of the information and illustration material that forms the basis of this book. We are particularly grateful for the gracious permission of Her Majesty the Queen for the use made of material from the Royal Archives, and specifically the photographs on pages 22, top, and 28.

Picture Credits: British Aerospace: 67. *Flight* pictures supplied by Quadrant Picture Library: 24, top; 26, top; 27, bottom; 31, left; 37, top; 44; 107; 125, top; 131; 136. Imperial War Museum: 134. Quadrant Picture Library, BAC photograph: 124, bottom; 141. Quadrant Picture Library, HSA photograph: 27, centre. The Queen's Flight: 38; 71, bottom; 82; 83, top; 83, bottom; 84, bottom; 84-5; 86; 87; 88; 114; 118; 119; 123; 127. Roger King Graphic Studios (Blandford Press copyright): 81; 103; 120; 133.

The majority of the remaining illustrations were taken for *Flight* and *The Aeroplane* and are held by the Quadrant Picture Library. Every effort has been made to trace the copyright holder of material and the Publishers apologise if it has not been possible to do so.